Retirement Shock

The Real Reason Retirement Feels Empty—And a Step-by-Step Guide to a Life That Matters

David John Cook

Dedication

To my sons, Ryan and Brandon—

I love you more than words can ever express. You are my greatest joy and my proudest legacy. I wish you lives filled with love, meaning, health, laughter, and purpose.

To my wife, Suzanne—

Thank you for always standing by me, supporting my wild ideas without hesitation, and sharing in every deep conversation, laugh, and quiet moment. I love you.

And to the millions of people stepping into retirement—

This book is for you.

May it be a compass when the confetti settles, and the deeper questions begin. May it help you navigate the unexpected space between freedom and purpose and inspire you to thrive in all the days still to come.

📍 Preface: The Shock No One Warned You About

This book is for anyone who has spent years showing up on job sites, in offices, in classrooms, on the road, or in scrubs. Whether you were running a team, turning a wrench, or making sure the mail got delivered, if you worked hard and gave your best, this book is for you.

Because here's the truth: retirement isn't always what you were promised.

You've probably been told it's the reward. The finish line. The long-deserved vacation after a life of hard work. But if you've recently retired—or are thinking about it—and feel a little off, a little lost, maybe even a little guilty about not loving it, you're not alone. You're not broken. You're just discovering what so many others do quietly: **retirement can feel empty.**

That was my shock.

After a long, successful career leading businesses that tackled major problems— from background credentialing to post 9/11 homeland security projects—I thought I had it figured out. I'd earned my success, earned my financial freedom, and even earned a degree from Oxford just for the challenge. But when the work faded and the calendar cleared, I hit a wall. I didn't miss the job. I missed who I was while doing it.

That's why I wrote this book.

Not to pitch another financial plan. Not to convince you to travel more or take up golf (unless you want to). I wrote it because I needed something I couldn't find: a real-world, relatable guide to how to feel like yourself again, or maybe, for the first time.

Out of that search came the Retirement Transition Framework (RTF)—a practical, human-centered roadmap for navigating the emotional, psychological, and identity shifts that come when the job ends. It doesn't matter whether you wore a tie or steel-toe boots—if you're asking, "What now?", this book has something for you.

You'll find stories—mine and others. Tools. Reflections. And maybe a few laughs. Because retirement can be hilarious, awkward, frustrating, and deeply fulfilling— sometimes all in the same day.

My goal? Not to impress you. Not to sell you on a lifestyle. But to walk with you, side by side, through this next phase—with honesty, clarity, and a plan.

Let's get real about retirement. Let's talk about the shock.

And more importantly, let's talk about what comes next.

Let's begin.

Table of Contents

Chapter 7

Offers strategies for reconnecting with family, friends, and communities, fostering meaningful connections in retirement.

Chapter 8

Shows how to leave your mark—through family, wisdom, or giving back—so your legacy lives on long after the job ends.

Chapter 9

Guides retirees on how to embrace digital tools for communication, learning, and staying connected in the modern world.

Chapter 10

Emphasizes maintaining physical, mental, and spiritual health in retirement through fitness, nutrition, and mindfulness.

Chapter 11

Concludes with how I used the RTF to design my retirement plan, sharing my experiences and those of others to inspire readers.

Appendix

- Academic Citations
- Media Citations
- Institutional References
- Referenced Technologies and Apps
- Glossary of Key Terms
- Top 20 Lessons from Retirement Shock
- Tool: Retirement Transition Framework (RTF) Summary Worksheet

Introduction: Transitioning from Career to Retirement

What You'll Learn:

It's not just about leaving a job—it's about figuring out who you are now. This chapter opens with real stories, surprising stats, and the tough questions that follow retirement.

You'll discover why the first step to reinvention is understanding what truly gives your life meaning—and how the Retirement Transition Framework (RTF) can guide that transformation.

"Don't simply retire from something; have something to retire to"
— Harry Emerson Fosdick

How the heck did I end up here? I thought to myself, sitting across from a room full of medical doctors and PhDs at the Centers for Disease Control (CDC). It was just days after 9/11, and the country was still reeling from the deadliest attack on our country. *Time Magazine* had already labeled it *"the bloodiest day on American soil since our Civil War,"* but now, another crisis was unfolding—one that most of the country didn't even know about yet. Anthrax had been found in U.S. post offices, including one in Trenton, NJ. Nine employees were exposed. Two tragically died. The CDC was scrambling to contain what appeared to be a biological terror attack, and somehow, our company was in the middle of it.

My partner Don and I didn't have backgrounds in homeland security. But there we were—two business guys suddenly part of a serious national crisis, asked to contribute to the response effort. I felt a surge of pride at being part of something that mattered, but also an unsettling realization: we were in uncharted territory. And looking back, I realized that's where I often did my best work—navigating the unknown.

What made my career especially engaging was the mix of solving complex problems and building new ventures in fast-moving environments. It challenged me in ways I didn't always expect—and kept me learning.

Why I Wrote This Book

If you've ever felt unsure or overwhelmed about retirement—you're in the right place. At my core, I'm just like you. I worked hard, provided for my family, and spent years focused on what's next. If you've ever laid awake thinking about how to support your loved ones, build a meaningful career, or figure out what comes after all the hard work—we already have something in common.

I also studied psychology, which means I tend to overanalyze life transitions. Yeah, I am that guy. That curiosity helped me realize something most retirement books ignore: **retirement isn't just a financial shift—it's a psychological one**. Writing this book gave me the chance to blend what I know from behavioral science with my own lived experience. I wanted to understand why retirement feels so shaky for many—and how we can move forward with clarity and purpose.

My career became a big part of my identity. I spent most of my life in business, helping companies grow and solve major customer challenges. But before that, I had my share of everyday jobs—detailing cars, cleaning university buildings, putting books away in the library. prepping fried chicken. I wasn't great at those jobs—I've always been a bit of a klutz. My mom used to joke, "Did you get any breading on the chicken, or just on yourself?" Still, I've always taken pride in an honest day's work, no matter the role—and that's always mattered to me.

And that's the point—it doesn't matter if you were a teacher, nurse, landscaper, bus driver, or CEO. If you showed up, gave your best, and took pride in your work, then we're alike. So, when that chapter ends, it's only natural to ask: *Who was I without the career that once defined me?*

That's what this book is about—not just retiring from work, but rewiring your life for meaning, connection, and joy. If you're anything like me, you don't just want to stop working—you want to start living differently.

Long before I retired, I got an early taste of how fragile our sense of identity can be—and how humility often shows up when you least expect it.

I had just been asked to lead a new team. The day before our first big meeting, I had a crown placed on one of my front teeth. No big deal... until I stood up to introduce myself, opened with a confident "Hello everyone," and about five words in—my crown popped off and bounced the entire length of the conference room table.

It was like a slow-motion movie. All eyes followed it. There I was, suddenly missing a front tooth, trying to maintain any shred of credibility while looking like I'd lost 50 IQ points. I finished the meeting with a bright red face and a whole new appreciation for humility. But here's the funny part: that team probably remembered me better than if I'd given the best speech of my life.

And that's something retirement teaches you too—it's not about being flawless. It's about being real.

Early in my retirement, I thought volunteering would be the answer. But when I ended up giving tours of nursing homes to anxious families, I felt like I was staring into my future. It wasn't purpose—it was a punch in the gut. I knew I needed something more.

That moment made me pause and wonder if others were feeling the same way.

Turns out, I wasn't alone. The more retirees I spoke with, the more I heard the same thing: we don't just lose our routines—we lose our identity, and no one prepares you for that. That's what pushed me to dig deeper—to find tools, strategies, and stories that could turn this confusing phase into something exciting.

An astonishing number of retirees feel this way—but few talk about it. The numbers are eye-opening:

✦ **One in three** retirees feels a significant **loss of identity**.

✦ **Over 40%** say they're **unhappy**, often because they can't find a renewed sense of direction.

✦ **Retirement can increase the risk of clinical depression by 40%.**

* Sources: Psychological Science (PMC8985220) and the Institute of Economic Affairs (2013) both report that retirement can reduce purpose and increase the risk of depression by up to 40%

That's why I'm sharing my journey. Not to offer a perfect solution, but to show you that if you're asking, "What now?"—you're not alone.

Retirement gets sold as a reward—beaches, wine glasses, and freedom. But the real version? It's more like standing in Home Depot on a Tuesday morning wondering why you're staring at power tools you've never used. It's weird. It's disorienting. And it's also a golden opportunity—if you know how to approach it.

Letting go of your job is hard. Whether you spent decades fixing plumbing, managing teams, or writing code—this is about rediscovering who you are *beyond* the job.

The stories, research, and expert advice in this book helped me through that process—and I hope they'll help you too. This isn't just another retirement book. It's a guide to redefining success on your own terms, reigniting your passions, and building a life that feels meaningful again.

I won't pretend to have all the answers. Your journey will be uniquely yours. But what I do know is this: reinvention is possible at any age. Whether you're letting go, starting over, or just craving something new—you're not alone. The best chapter of your life may be right around the corner. Let's find it together.

How Risk Became My Career—and My Training Ground for Reinvention

I think it would be disingenuous to recommend the ideas in this book without sharing my own story—and being vulnerable in the process. That's why I do it here, and throughout the chapters that follow.

I didn't set out to work in risk management—it found me. My dad helped me land a job as a management trainee with a company that gathered medical and investigative data for life insurance underwriting. The pay wasn't great, but I was grateful to start working right out of college.

I had no idea that role would lead to a decades-long career in risk management—at levels I never could've imagined. Honestly, I was just a guy from Bloomington, Illinois. No roadmap—just a strong work ethic and a willingness to keep learning.

As time went on, I helped clients navigate some of their most complex challenges—everything from compliance concerns to post 9/11 security needs. These environments required clarity and quick thinking, which pushed me to grow.

I had the opportunity to work with talented teams, facing challenges that required urgency and creativity. Those moments taught me the value of collaboration under pressure. These weren't just job responsibilities—they were defining issues of the time that called for collaboration and purposeful action. A few that stand out:

- ✦ **Negligent Hiring Liability:** Corporations needed to reduce legal exposure from bad hires—prompting adoption of large-scale employee screening solutions.

- ✦ **Military Medical Readiness Gaps:** In response to the Gulf War, the Army Reserve needed a rapid medical compliance program to ensure deployability and statutory readiness.

- ✦ **Post-9/11 Bioterrorism Threats:** Homeland Security required urgent national preparedness efforts to address emerging bioterror risks, including anthrax, smallpox and SARS exposure.
- ✦ **Vendor-Related Lawsuits in Real Estate:** The apartment industry faced rising liability from third-party contractors leading to the implementation of vendor credentialing systems.
- ✦ **Airport Screening Crisis Post 9/11:** With the government federalizing airport security, the TSA urgently needed to screen and onboard 100,000 agents in record time.

What connected all these? Credentialing. We used technology and data to evaluate people against requirements, reducing risk and increasing confidence. That strategy—structured, data-driven, and purpose-oriented—became the model for every business I started or helped scale.

And here's the connection: that same mindset applies to retirement.

This book offers a framework to help you approach retirement with intention. We often think planning stops at finances—but it doesn't. Without structure, even a good situation can feel unstable.

From Purpose to Pivot – Lessons from a Life in Risk

For decades, my work moved at a relentless pace—driven by customer urgency and the constant pressure to deliver profitable growth. You'd think I would've been counting down the days to retirement—and trust me, I was. But stepping away from that intensity wasn't easy. Still, the lessons I learned during those years helped prepare me for what came next—and they've become the foundation for everything you'll find in this book.

I remember working with a national real estate group that managed thousands of multi-family housing units. Lawsuits were rising—often tied to vendors and subcontractors who hadn't been properly vetted. So, we pitched something different: a credentialing system that used data to verify vendor insurance, background checks, and compliance before they ever set foot on a property.

One incident drove the point home. A stair repair vendor was hired to fix a squeaky and loose staircase between the third and fourth floors of a building. He set up a ladder underneath the stairs, began his work, and at some point, slipped, falling off the ladder and down the metal and concrete staircase. Tragically, he was killed. His insurance had expired, but no one caught it before he arrived. The vendor's family sued the apartment owners and won a significant settlement—even though the owners hadn't done anything wrong. They simply didn't have a system in place to catch the risk ahead of time.

Before that, most vendors were 'cleared' manually—a patchwork of paper files, verbal confirmations, and missed expiration dates. It was fraught with mistakes. In fact, some vendors with serious criminal histories were never screened at all. A few even went on to assault tenants—incidents that could've been prevented with a basic background check.

Credentialing wasn't just about reducing liability. It was about building safety, accountability, and trust into the system. When done right, it protected everyone: tenants, vendors, and the property owners themselves.

That project stuck with me. Because it reminded me that meaningful change doesn't always come from saving the day—it often comes from quietly building something that lasts. As I transitioned into retirement, that mindset followed me. I didn't want to stop doing meaningful work. I just needed to redirect it.

Let me share another example of how quickly risk can shift.

During that time, the work we were doing drew national attention. I'll never forget opening an edition of *The New York Times* and seeing a photo of me with a quote. It wasn't about recognition—it was a reminder that the moment was real, and the stakes were high. What we were doing truly mattered.

Just three days after 9/11, I got a call from a major pharmaceutical company. Ten of their computer engineering employees—all Middle Eastern descent—had called in sick and vanished. Their homes were empty. The company was in full-blown panic.

"Should we recheck the criminal records of all 30,000 employees?" the Senior Vice President of HR asked me. That kind of mass re-screening was unprecedented at the time. There were real fears: Had malicious code been planted? Could critical drug formulas have been altered?

In the end, nothing malicious was found. But the fear was real—and it exposed just how vulnerable even well-run organizations could be when trust is shaken. My job wasn't just about logistics—it was about helping people stay grounded in moments of chaos.

My experiences taught me something powerful: resilience, adaptability, and teamwork matter most in moments of pressure—even the quiet kind. And oddly enough, those same traits became just as important when I retired—when the external demands faded, and the internal questions began.

Expert Insight: The Psychological Impact of Retirement

Dr. Nancy Schlossberg, a psychologist who has studied the transitions people face throughout life, explains, *"Retirement is not just a financial decision; it's a psychological journey. It's about finding new ways to feel useful, valued, and connected."*

This resonates deeply with my experience. Retirement wasn't just about managing my time; it was a deeper struggle with my identity and emotions. I had spent decades defining myself through my work and letting go felt like losing a part of who I was. Reimagining fulfillment and understanding my place in this new chapter proved to be more challenging than I anticipated.

But it's these challenges that have ultimately shaped my journey and my desire to share what I've learned.

Letting go of your work identity is no joke. At one point, I caught myself giving a PowerPoint-style update to my wife about our weekend plans. I even used bullet points. She was not impressed and just laughed at me. It turns out old habits die hard!

The Unexpected Challenge of Retirement: Who Am I Now?

At 55, I *thought* I was one of the lucky ones. I had built a successful career, reached financial stability, and had the opportunity to retire early. But then, almost overnight, everything that had once given me a sense of purpose from my job came to a sudden halt. The excitement, the structure, and the thrill of working toward something meaningful was gone, and with it, my sense of identity.

Had I planned to retire at 55? Not exactly. The decision wasn't something I agonized over for years. Like many, I had always figured I would know when the time was right. In some ways, the timing felt logical—financially, I was prepared, and I had spent decades planning for and hoping for this moment. But what I didn't anticipate was *how* retirement would feel once I stepped away. The truth is, no matter how much planning you do, there's an emotional side to retirement that no spreadsheet or financial planner can fully prepare you for.

For me, retirement wasn't just a financial milestone; it was a complete shift in identity. My kids were grown, my career was behind me, and for the first time in decades, I had to ask myself: *What now?*

Suzanne and I traveled to many countries, and while those adventures were fun and interesting, they didn't fill the void. I even enrolled at Oxford University, eager to challenge myself in a new way, immersing myself in an environment where intellectual rigor and debate sharpened my thinking. But when that chapter ended— when the classes were done, the exams completed—I found myself in the same place, staring at the same unsettling question: *What's next?*

Sure, pickleball, golf, and poolside afternoons are great—they're good for your health, good for your soul, and its great socializing. But let's be honest: they aren't a reinvention of purpose. They're hobbies, not a roadmap for the next chapter of life. I needed something deeper,

something that provided a real sense of contribution and meaning beyond just filling my time.

This is a dilemma many retirees face, yet few openly talk about it. We spend our lives working toward retirement as if it's the ultimate finish line, the reward we've earned after decades of effort. But what happens when you cross that line and realize nothing is waiting on the other side? I had assumed retirement was about stepping back, finally having the time to relax. But I've since learned that it's really about stepping *forward*—into something new, something that gives life meaning beyond work.

So, when is the right time to retire? That's a personal decision, and the answer isn't just about money, although we will discuss this in Chapter 2—it's about knowing what you're retiring *to*, not just what you're retiring *from*.

It's easy to think that once you hit your financial target, you're ready. But I've learned that financial security is just the foundation. What matters just as much is having a plan for how you'll spend your time, what will give you a renewed sense of direction, and how you'll continue to grow.

For me, that realization came *after* I had already stepped into retirement. I hadn't given enough thought to what would replace the sense of fulfillment I got from my work. And so, I began searching—through travel, through education, through hobbies—all to rediscover a version of myself that felt whole again.

If you're reading this and wondering when the right time is for *you*, my advice is this: Don't just plan for the day you retire—plan for the days *after* you retire. The best retirement isn't about doing nothing. It's about transformation. It's about discovering new passions, a new identity, and ultimately, a new purpose.

Reframing Uncertainty as an Opportunity

Retirement can feel overwhelming at first. One minute, you've got a structured routine—the emails, the calls, the meetings, the sense of being needed. And then, suddenly, it all stops. The first day of retirement felt strangely quiet. I remember waking up at the same time I always had, almost on autopilot, before realizing I had nowhere to be. Just a wide-open day staring back at me.

At first, that freedom felt like a luxury. I played pickleball, read the news a little longer over coffee, and even went to the beach in the afternoon just because I could. But by the end of that first week, something felt off. The silence that once seemed peaceful started feeling empty. The space where my work used to be—the structure, the purpose, the momentum—was now just a void.

That's when the doubts started creeping in. *Had I made a mistake? Was I ready for this?* I had spent decades mastering my career, finding meaning in my work, and suddenly, it felt like none of it mattered anymore. And while I knew logically that I had *earned* this time, emotionally, I felt unmoored. The transition from being highly productive to having no defined role was jarring in a way I hadn't anticipated.

I tried to stay busy, taking on small projects and convincing myself that staying occupied was the key. But the truth is, I wasn't looking for *more activities*—I was looking for *meaning*.

That's when I started to shift my perspective. Instead of seeing the uncertainty as something to fear, I began to see it as an opportunity. A blank slate can be daunting, but it can also be exciting. It's a chance to finally do all those things I never had time for before—to learn, to grow, to redefine what success means on my own terms.

Have you asked yourself: What will this next chapter truly look like for me? The uncertainty can be uncomfortable, even unsettling. There were moments when I felt completely out of my depth, questioning whether I had anything valuable to offer outside of my past career. But that discomfort ended up being the doorway to a lot more fulfillment than I ever expected.

Let's be real though—it's not always easy. Reinventing yourself takes work and resilience. And as you'll see throughout this book, many retirees face these same challenges. That's exactly why I developed a framework to guide this transformation—a way to navigate this transition with purpose and direction.

But before we dive into that, I want to take a step back—because my journey to finding meaning in retirement didn't start on the day I walked away from my career. Like so many it started much earlier, in the delicate balancing act of building both a professional legacy *and* a meaningful family life. Because while finding purpose in retirement is crucial, the real challenge is making sure that, along the way, you haven't lost sight of the things that matter most.

Balancing the Demands of Career and Family

Retirement isn't just about leaving the workforce—it often coincides with another life-changing shift: the empty nest. For years, work and family responsibilities shaped my identity, filling my days with purpose, structure, and a sense of being needed. Then sequentially both began to fade. The emails stopped, the meetings disappeared, and at home, the once-busy house grew quieter. It was my *double whammy*. I had spent decades building a career while raising my sons, and suddenly, both roles—the ones that had defined me—were no longer at the center of my daily life.

Does this apply to you as well? Have you found yourself navigating not just the end of a career, but also the shift in your family dynamics? If so, you're not alone. Many of us enter retirement thinking we're just stepping away from work, only to realize we're also stepping into a new phase of family life. It's a transition that can feel unsettling, but it's also an opportunity—one that requires reflection, adjustment, and a fresh perspective on what truly gives life meaning.

For me, that reflection led back to one of the most important roles I've ever had: being a father. Despite a demanding career, I made it a point to be there—at the games, the concerts, the school projects, every milestone, the moments that mattered. Raising my sons, Ryan and Brandon, with my first wife wasn't just a role—it was the heart of who I was.

I was their biggest fan (still am)—cheering from the sidelines and showing up when it counted. That time together grounded me in ways no business meeting ever could. I refused to let my career take precedence over being their father. The moments that mattered most were the ones when they looked to me for guidance, support, or simply to see a familiar face in the crowd. I'll never forget the time Brandon waved me down from the La Crosse field—just to show me his collarbone, bent in half. Yikes—not that I want my kids hurt! But those were the moments that truly kept me anchored.

Balancing the demands of a career and fatherhood was my identity. Yet, like of many of you the reality of that balancing act was often grueling. The constant travel, late nights, and pressures of my job left me exhausted in ways that went far beyond physical fatigue. There were times when I questioned if it was all worth it, wondering if the sacrifices were too high. But my drive to protect, provide, and succeed never wavered.

Yes, financial success was part of the journey, but the real wealth was in the bond I shared with my sons. I took immense pride in the fact that, despite the sacrifices, I managed to be present for them. There were plenty of times I had to reroute flights or drive to another town just to make it home in time. But as fathers—and mothers—

we do what it takes. Balancing both worlds—executive and father—often felt like walking a tightrope. Still, I wouldn't trade those years for anything. They taught me that success isn't just measured by career accomplishments; it's also found in the love, support, and presence you give to those who matter most.

As I transitioned into retirement, I quickly realized that the balance I had worked so hard to maintain was no longer the same. The career that had demanded my time and energy had ended, and my children were grown, leaving me to confront an unfamiliar reality. This shift was not only about finding new activities to fill my time, but about redefining who I was without those dual roles to anchor me. The psychological impact of stepping away from both career and family obligations was profound and challenging.

The Retirement Surge: What's Coming Next

Think you're the only one struggling with the psychological impact of retirement? Trust me—you're not alone. Think it won't happen to you when the time comes? I genuinely hope it doesn't. But let's revisit the numbers: one in three retirees experiences a significant loss of identity. Over 40% say they're unhappy—often because they can't find a renewed sense of direction. And retirement can increase the risk of clinical depression by 40%.

What makes this even more pressing is that the personal challenges I faced (and hopefully you won't) are the same one's millions of others will soon encounter. Over the next decade, approximately 76 million people in the U.S. will reach retirement age—creating one of the most significant demographic shifts in our history. While many will embrace the freedom retirement offers, countless others will find themselves navigating uncertainty, identity loss, and the search for a new sense of purpose. And given how fast this group is growing, the emotional toll? You can do the math.

This isn't a new phenomenon—it's part of an evolving pattern. Look at the trends over the past few decades: ten years ago, about 10,000 people reached retirement age every single day. That number hasn't slowed—it's only grown.

The Baby Boomer generation is redefining what retirement looks like, driving the largest workforce shift in history. More people than ever are facing this transition, yet few are truly prepared for what lies beyond the financial planning. The pace is accelerating—and what comes after the paycheck is where the real challenge begins.

What about the *age* of retirement? Historically, the average retirement age hovered around 62 for decades, but as life expectancy and financial realities have changed, so have retirement patterns. Today, more people are working longer—whether by necessity or choice—with the average age creeping up to 64 or 65. Yet at the same time, some are opting for early retirement, influenced by financial independence movements, corporate buyouts, economic changes or personal circumstances.

These shifting demographics mean we're entering uncharted territory. With more retirees than ever before, we're witnessing a fundamental change in what retirement looks like. Unlike past generations, where retirement was often a brief period of rest after a lifetime of labor, today's retirees are healthier, more active, and facing decades of post-career life. That extended time brings both opportunity and challenge—the opportunity to reinvent oneself, but also the challenge of navigating an identity shift that previous generations may not have faced in the same way.

These are not just numbers; these are people with diverse backgrounds—teachers, bus drivers, CEOs, salespeople, restaurant managers, accountants, soldiers, factory workers, and healthcare professionals. They're people who, like me, will need to grapple with redefining success once their traditional roles come to an end. This looming wave of retirees highlights the urgent need for practical guidance, emotional support, and frameworks to help navigate life after work.

Understanding where you fit into this larger trend can be powerful. It's not just *your* journey—it's a collective experience shared by millions. And while the challenges are real, so is the potential to shape this next phase into something fulfilling and meaningful.

Redefining Identity: From Retirement Confusion to Purpose

The Identity Questions That Keep You Up at Night

For years, I had a clear answer when someone asked, *what do you do?* My job, my responsibilities, my industry —it all rolled off the tongue effortlessly. Like the time I ran into an old colleague at the grocery store. He was in a rush, talking about how slammed he was at work, deadlines piling up, big deals in the pipeline. Then he turned to me with that polite, almost-too-cheerful tone: *So, what are you up to these days?*

I hesitated. For a second, I considered spinning something impressive. Instead, I went with the truth: *Oh, just figuring out this retirement thing.*

He nodded, gave me that polite smile, and said, *must be nice,* before rushing off to his next meeting. I stood there in the produce aisle, holding a bag of apples, feeling like I had just been benched from the game of life. That simple conversation stuck with me. It wasn't just awkward—it exposed something deeper. Without a job title, I wasn't sure who I was anymore.

The more I thought about retirement, the more I felt this weight in my chest. A vague unease, like I was missing something important. Sure, the days lost their structure—and their usual chaos. That should've felt freeing. But without the thrill of closing a deal or building a company, I started to wonder: Is this really it? There had to be more.

Then there are the *awkward* moments—the subtle but jarring experiences that remind you just how much life has shifted. Like a recent trip to the doctor for my annual physical. Filling out the medical forms used to be easy—quick checkmarks down the page. This time, I had to pause, mark "yes" on a few boxes, and explain. It was a subtle reminder that time was moving on. And under 'Occupation,' I stared at the blank space. For years, I knew exactly what to write. But now? *Retired.* The word felt... final. Like I had been filed away into a different category of existence. Did retirement also mean declining health?

The Challenge of Showing Up as a 'Retiree'

There's also a subtle pressure in how you *show up* as a retiree. What do I mean? Some people expect you to be endlessly relaxed, embracing hobbies and vacations with ease. Others assume you're *done* contributing, as if retirement means stepping back rather than stepping into something new.

At my lowest points, I kept asking myself:

✦ *Should I be doing something more productive? Maybe even making money?*

✦ *Am I wasting this time when I could be helping someone?*

✦ *Why does everyone else seem to have figured this out while I'm still struggling?*

✦ *Is this what the rest of life looks like—unstructured days, surface-level conversations, and hobbies that don't quite fill the void?*

There was a particular evening when it hit me hardest. I was sitting outside by the pool, Chardonnay in hand (yeah, it's the drink my friends love to tease me about), watching the sunset. Everything looked perfect—but inside, I felt empty. I had worked my whole life to reach this point, and yet, I felt more lost than ever.

Reinventing Myself: Finding a New Purpose

Then it hit me: retirement isn't just an ending or an invitation to play—it's a blank page, and a chance to reset how we see ourselves. But unlike every chapter before, this one doesn't come with a clear roadmap. That's what makes it both terrifying and exhilarating. There's no job title to chase, no promotions to earn, just the question: What do I want this next phase to be about?

Psychologists call this kind of transition a *role exit*—a shift in identity that happens when we leave behind a major part of who we were. Just like new parents adjust to life with a child, or soldiers transition back to civilian life, retirees must redefine themselves in a world where their previous roles no longer apply. And like any major transition, this process can bring both excitement and anxiety. The key is not to let the uncertainty paralyze you but to use it as an invitation to explore what's next.

I knew staying busy wasn't enough. I wanted meaning, not just motion. So, I started exploring—writing, volunteering, mentoring. ach step felt like a small experiment— testing what might come next. And slowly, something began to shift. The more I leaned into new experiences, the more I realized that purpose wasn't something I had left behind in my career—it was something I could create again, in a new way. I wasn't chasing a new identity—I was building a life that felt whole again.

I didn't realize it at the time, but those early struggles were leading me toward something important. I wasn't just losing my old identity—I was making space for a new one. It wasn't about staying busy for the sake of it; it was about finding something that truly mattered. Something that made me excited to get up in the morning again.

Retirement isn't about fading into the background. It's about rising into something new—redefining success on your own terms and giving yourself permission to grow in ways you hadn't even imagined.

Introducing the Retirement Transition Framework (RTF)

When most people think about retirement, their first question is: *Can I afford to retire?* It's a crucial question, and financial security is undeniably important. But financial readiness is just the foundation—it's not the full picture. Retirement is more than a numbers game; it's a major life transition that impacts your identity, sense of purpose, and daily structure. You can have all the money you need and still feel lost without a clear plan for what comes next.

That's where the Retirement Transition Framework (RTF) comes in.

Throughout my career, I faced challenges that demanded strategic thinking, adaptability, and problem-solving. When I entered retirement, I realized those same skills could guide me through this unfamiliar chapter. But while financial tools helped prepare me for retirement on paper, I found there was no roadmap for the emotional, psychological, and social side of the journey. So, I developed the Retirement Transition Framework (RTF) to bridge that gap—a structured, human-centered approach that helps make the non-financial side of retirement just as intentional as the financial.

Why the RTF is Necessary

Traditional retirement planning often zeroes in on financial security—but that's just one piece of the puzzle. The RTF recognizes that retirement is a multifaceted experience, requiring more than just a solid balance sheet. By addressing the emotional, psychological, and social shifts that come with this transition, the RTF offers a fuller picture of what it takes to truly thrive in this next chapter.

As I like to say, *it helps you not just fill your days—but feel your days.*

Applying the RTF

Throughout this book, we'll be applying the RTF to real-life scenarios and case studies. We'll explore how the framework can be used to navigate the challenges of retirement and create a fulfilling life. By the end of this book, you'll have a clear understanding of how to apply the RTF to your own life and create a personalized plan for your retirement transition.

How the RTF Works

The framework is a 9-step framework that guides you through the retirement transition process. Each step builds on the previous one, providing a clear and structured approach to navigating the challenges of retirement.

RTF Step	Focus	Description
Step 1: Financial Stability as the Foundation		Retirement freedom starts with financial security. This step ensures your finances are in order so you can focus on purpose, fulfillment, and growth.
Step 2: Letting Go of Old Identities & Embracing Change		Your career was part of who you were—but it's not all you are. This step helps you shift from a work-centered identity to an expanded sense of self.
Step 3: Redefining Success & Finding Fulfillment		This step helps redefine what a meaningful, fulfilling retirement looks like for you.
Step 4: Exploring New Passions & Purpose		Retirement is an opportunity to reignite curiosity. This step guides you in identifying passions, hobbies, or work that give life deeper meaning.
Step 5: Strengthening Relationships & Social Connections		Without workplace interactions, social circles often shrink. This step helps you build strong relationships and stay connected in retirement.
Step 6: Adapting to Technology & Lifelong Learning		Technology isn't just for the next generation—it's for you. This step shows how digital tools can keep you engaged, informed, and empowered.
Step 7: Prioritizing Health & Well-Being		Physical, mental, and spiritual health shape quality of life. This step focuses on fitness, nutrition, mindfulness, and longevity strategies.
Step 8: Leaving a Legacy – Making a Lasting Impact		Retirement is your chance to contribute to something bigger than yourself. This step focuses on sharing wisdom, giving back, and creating a meaningful legacy that outlives you.
Step 9: RTF in Action – My Plan in Motion		A personal story that brings the Retirement Transition Framework to life. This step shares how I applied the RTF and the results it created in my own retirement journey.

The Retirement Transition Framework (RTF) is designed to tackle retirement one piece at a time.

Each step helps take that "what now?" feeling and turn it into something real, actionable, and doable—with stories, expert insights, and reflection prompts to guide you along the way.

Here's the deal: the RTF gives you a clear path to reboot. And the skills you've built over a lifetime—like grit, adaptability, and problem-solving—are exactly what you need now. You're not starting over; you're building something new. Like me, it's your chance to move forward instead of looking back. That's what this book is here to help with—finding a direction that truly feels like you.

As I said earlier, this isn't your typical retirement book about how to stretch your 401(k). It's about what comes after the money stuff—rediscovering who you are, what excites you, and what gives your life meaning now.

Chapter 1 Takeaways: Retirement Is More Than a Paycheck—It's a New Identity

- ☑ **Retirement is not just a financial milestone—it's a psychological transition.** The loss of structure, status, and purpose can leave you feeling unmoored, even if you're financially prepared.

- ☑ **You're not alone in feeling uncertain.** One in three retirees experience's identity loss. Over 40% feel unhappy or aimless in retirement—not because of money, but because of meaning.

- ☑ **It's okay to feel lost before you feel found.** Reinvention doesn't happen overnight. Real purpose takes time, exploration, and intention, not just keeping busy.

- ☑ **The Retirement Transition Framework (RTF) starts here.** This first chapter lays the foundation for a new kind of retirement—one that's built on clarity, resilience, and reinvention.

- ☑ **You're not retiring from life—you're rewiring for a new one.** The RTF helps you answer: *Who am I now?* and *What's next?*—so your next chapter becomes your best chapter.

That said, we can't skip the money part. If your financial foundation isn't solid, it's hard to focus on purpose—I mean, you still gotta eat! So first, we'll check your financial base. If it's strong, great—let's roll. If not, no stress. The next chapter will help you get it on track.

Then we'll dive into the good stuff—your next chapter, built with intention, curiosity, and the RTF as your guide.

By the end of this journey, you'll have your own personalized plan for retirement—one that gives you both the freedom and the purpose to make this next phase of life truly matter.

Because the RTF isn't just a tool—it's your roadmap to a life with meaning.

Managing Your Finances – Achieving Financial Stability in Retirement

What you will learn: Financial security is your foundation. Without it, everything else in retirement is harder to build.

"Retirement is when you stop living at work and start working at living... but somehow, your money decides to retire faster than you do." - Unknown

1. The Harsh Reality of Retirement Readiness

Did you know?

Nearly half (45%) of retirees have less than $100,000 saved, with only 25% feeling confident about their financial security. This highlights a stark reality: retirement readiness is a widespread concern.

Source: Employee Benefit Research Institute & Insured Retirement Institute

These numbers highlight a stark reality: retirement readiness is a major concern. But the bigger question isn't just how much you've saved—it's whether your savings will last for the decades ahead. Retirement planning isn't about hitting a single number; it's about building financial security and flexibility for the long term.

2. Financial Stability is Your Foundation

Financial stability isn't just nice—it's essential. Without it, even the best retirement plans can fall apart, leaving you stressed rather than enjoying your retirement years.

Financial stability enables life reinvention. It allows you to handle life's unexpected transitions—whether divorce, medical events, or shifting priorities—with confidence. Retirement isn't simply about money; it's about your ability to reinvent your life when circumstances change.

In this chapter, we'll explore practical ways to secure your finances, handle surprises, and build a foundation that lets you enjoy retirement confidently.

3. Lessons from the Trenches

I've seen firsthand how financial instability can derail even the most well-intentioned retirement plans. I've had friends who assumed their pensions and Social Security checks would be enough, only to realize—far too late—that medical expenses, inflation, and unexpected costs quickly drained their savings. And I've met others who planned meticulously, making strategic moves that allowed them to step into retirement with confidence, ready to embrace their next chapter without the constant stress of money hanging over their heads.

Think of financial stability as laying the groundwork for a new, exciting chapter of your life. Without this solid foundation, the structure of your retirement will always feel fragile. But with it, you can build something strong, purposeful, and fulfilling.

Jim's Wake Up Call

Take Jim, for example—a 67-year-old retiree who thought he had done everything right. He had a pension, some savings, and an adequate Social Security check. However, rising healthcare costs and inflation quickly eroded his financial security. At first, he shrugged off the higher bills—cut back on dining out, postponed a trip. But then, one night, as he sat at the kitchen table staring at his dwindling savings, a sinking feeling hit him.

"Is this it?" he thought. "Did I work 40 years just to scrape by?"

That's when he knew something had to change. Eventually, Jim found a solution—he took on part-time consulting work, leveraging decades of experience to supplement his income. While he didn't expect to work in retirement, he realized that financial stability wasn't just about numbers—it was about peace of mind.

Jim's story is not unique. Many retirees face financial surprises that force them to rethink their plans. That's why this chapter will walk you through how to either address the need to generate extra income if necessary or turn income generation into a new passion. Either way, building financial stability gives you the freedom to address the other elephant in the room, which we'll discuss later: purpose, identity, and finding the new you in retirement.

Let me share my own experience, which taught me a valuable lesson about adaptability and resilience.

My Personal Lesson: Financial Recalibration

Jim's story exemplifies how unexpected financial shifts can reshape retirement. But sometimes, financial recalibration comes not from external forces like inflation but from deeply personal life transitions. I know this all too well. I had spent decades building what I thought was a rock-solid retirement plan—carefully saving, investing, and structuring my future with a long-term vision in mind. But life doesn't always unfold the way we expect.

Like many people, I never imagined I would go through a divorce. My first wife was a wonderful, caring person, and we spent many good years together. But over time, we grew apart, becoming different people with different goals. At some point, I had to acknowledge that a truly fulfilling second half of life—one filled with low stress, happiness, and purpose—meant making a difficult but necessary transition.

Divorce isn't just emotionally challenging; it's a financial earthquake. Overnight, half of everything I had built—our savings, investments, and assets—was gone. And I wouldn't have done it any other way. I'm a deeply loyal person, and ensuring my first wife was fully taken care of was never in question. But the reality was clear: my retirement plan needed a serious recalibration.

I remember sitting in my attorney's office, staring at the settlement papers. I had spent decades planning for retirement, but not for this. The financial spreadsheets I once relied on now felt meaningless. While I had no regrets, I had to adjust my expectations, reassess my financial stability, and rethink what my next phase of life would look like. I wasn't starting from scratch, but I was starting over. And that was a gut punch I never saw coming.

This experience reinforced something I now emphasize to anyone planning for retirement: Life happens. The unexpected will happen. And when it does, financial stability isn't just about numbers—it's about adaptability, resilience, and the ability to pivot without fear.

That's why this chapter isn't just about financial planning in theory—it's about preparing for the realities of retirement. Whether it's a divorce, a medical event, or a change in priorities, life in the second half is full of transitions. The key is having a financial foundation that allows you to navigate those changes with confidence. My divorce was an unexpected pivot, but it reinforced a key truth: Retirement isn't just about money. It's about reinvention.

My divorce reinforced a key truth: retirement isn't just about money—it's about the ability to reinvent yourself. Yet, financial struggles can leave some retirees feeling desperate and unsure about the future. To illustrate this point in a lighter context, let's consider an unusual scenario depicted in a popular film.

A Tale of Unexpected Financial Struggles

Imagine reaching retirement and finding out that the pension you counted on is suddenly gone. In the movie *Going in Style*, a group of retirees—played by Morgan Freeman, Michael Caine, and Alan Arkin—find themselves in that exact scenario. Faced with financial insecurity after their pensions disappear, they decide to take matters into their own hands in a rather unconventional way: they plan to rob a bank.

Retirement should be about enjoying your golden years—not scrambling to make ends meet. But for some retirees, financial struggles can feel so overwhelming that even a bank heist starts to sound logical. (Okay, I'm kidding—please don't rob a bank.) But the film highlights a very real issue: financial struggles in retirement can lead to desperation and unexpected decisions.

Thankfully, there are practical, less risky ways to address financial instability, even if the nest egg isn't as robust as hoped.

4. Why Financial Stability Matters in Retirement

Connection to the Retirement Transition Framework (RTF)

This book isn't about retirement finance—it's about the deeper emotional and psychological challenges that come with transitioning into retirement and how to create a fulfilling, purpose-driven life. However, financial stability is an essential first step in the **Retirement Transition Framework (RTF)** because without it, addressing these other aspects—purpose, identity, relationships, and personal growth—becomes significantly more difficult.

Worrying about money can overshadow everything else, making it hard to focus on building a meaningful retirement. It is the foundation that you build on in retirement to achieve your reinvention.

I wish I could say I retired with a spreadsheet so flawless it made my financial planner weep tears of joy. But the truth is, even with a solid plan, I still had doubts. Retirement is a leap, and no matter how much you've saved or how well you've budgeted, that first step can feel like stepping off a cliff and hoping your parachute is packed right!

That's why this chapter exists—not to make you a financial planner, but to help you build the financial stability needed to move into the next phase of life with confidence and peace of mind. It also explores ways to generate income in retirement—whether to cover financial gaps or, as many discover, to pursue a new entrepreneurial passion.

Either way, this chapter is filled with practical, actionable insights to strengthen your financial foundation, allowing you to focus on what truly matters in retirement.

Understanding the importance of financial stability is crucial. Now, let's shift gears and put theory into practice. In the next section, we'll evaluate your financial readiness and discuss practical strategies to build a stable foundation.

5. Building Financial Stability (practical strategies)

Let's make this personal now and ask the tough questions but also give you some benchmarks to compare. This section is a measure tool to assess where you are, but I won't leave you there. I also provided some of the same strategies I used to get where I wanted to be.

Have You Saved Enough for Retirement?

One of the biggest concerns for retirees is whether they have enough savings to last throughout retirement. But what does "enough" really mean? How do your savings compare to the average retiree? Let's break it down.

How Much Do Retirees Have Saved? (the Truth)

Let's quickly summarize key facts to see how you stack up against the average retiree:

- ✦ Median Retirement Savings (Age 65-74):
  $164,000 (Federal Reserve)
- ✦ Percentage of Retirees with Less Than $100,000 Saved:
  Nearly 50% (Employee Benefit Research Institute)
- ✦ Average Monthly Social Security Benefit:
  $1,900/month (~$22,800/year)
  Reality Check: Often insufficient to fully cover essential living expenses.

The Impact of Having (or Not Having) a Retirement Plan (A plan matters)

The gap in savings is even more dramatic when comparing those with and without a structured retirement plan (such as a 401(k) or IRA):

Workers Without a Retirement Plan:

- ✦ 71% have less than $10,000 in total savings and investments.
- ✦ The typical working household has a median retirement account balance of $2,500, while near-retirement households have a median of $14,500.

Retirees Without a Retirement Plan:

- ✦ 63% have less than $10,000 in savings.
- ✦ In contrast, only 8% of retirees with a retirement plan report such low savings.

Key Takeaway: Having a structured retirement plan dramatically improves financial security. Those without one are significantly more likely to struggle financially, reinforcing the importance of early and consistent planning.

How Much Should You Have Saved?
Retirement Savings Benchmarks

💰 How Much Should You Have Saved?

Now that we've looked at how most retirees are doing, let's talk about what financial experts recommend. How much is enough? Here are three common benchmarks to help you assess where you stand:

- ✦ **10x Salary Rule** – Save 10 times your final salary by age 67.
- ✦ **4% Rule** – Save 25x your desired annual income to safely withdraw 4% each year.
- ✦ **Reality Rule** – Aim for 15–20x your salary to account for healthcare, longevity, and market ups and downs.

Each of these depends on your lifestyle and goals. No single rule fits everyone, but they provide a useful range to assess where you stand.

Summary Table

Benchmark	Target Savings	Best For
10x Salary Rule	10× final salary	Modest lifestyle with Social Security support
4% Rule	25× annual expenses	Conservative savers seeking long-term security
Reality Rule	15–20× final salary	Balanced planning for flexibility and rising costs

- ☑ If you're on track or above these benchmarks, great—you have room to plan freely.
- ☑ If you're behind, don't panic. The next sections walk through smart, actionable ways to catch up, generate income, and create a plan that works for your situation.

Ensuring Your Funds Last in Retirement

With people living longer than ever, financial planning doesn't end once you reach your savings goal. The real challenge is making sure your money lasts. This requires smart withdrawals, balanced investments, and protection against inflation—so you can enjoy retirement without financial stress.

How to Withdraw Money in Retirement Without Running Out

A well-planned withdrawal strategy helps stretch your savings over your lifetime. Here are some simple ways to manage your withdrawals wisely:

- ☑ The 4% Rule (or a Flexible Version) – A simple rule of thumb: withdraw 3-4% of your total savings each year to help your money last. Adjust your withdrawals based on expenses and investment performance.
- ☑ The Bucket Strategy – Divide your savings into three "buckets" to balance risk and stability:
  - ✦ Short-term (1-3 years): Keep cash available for daily living expenses.
  - ✦ Mid-term (3-10 years): Invest in lower-risk options like bonds or dividend stocks for stability.
  - ✦ Long-term (10+ years): Keep a portion in stocks to ensure growth and outpace inflation.
- ☑ Adjusting Withdrawals for Market Changes (Dynamic Withdrawals) – If the stock market drops, withdraw less to avoid selling investments at a loss. In good years, you can increase withdrawals slightly.
- ☑ Required Minimum Distributions (RMDs) – If you have a 401(k) or IRA, the IRS requires you to start withdrawing a minimum amount by age 73 to avoid tax penalties.

Investing to Make Your Savings Last

To keep up with rising costs and avoid running out of money, retirees should not move all their savings into low-risk investments. A mix of safe and growth-oriented investments is key to long-term financial security.

- Stocks for Growth – Keeping 50-60% of your portfolio in stocks (if you're comfortable with some risk) can help your savings keep pace with inflation.

- Bonds & Fixed Income – Invest in bonds and Treasury Inflation-Protected Securities (TIPS) to provide stable, lower-risk income that adjusts for inflation.

- Annuities & Passive Income – Fixed annuities, dividend-paying stocks, and rental properties can create a steady, predictable income stream throughout retirement.

Protecting Your Money from Inflation & Rising Costs

Over a 30-year retirement, inflation can cut your buying power in half. That means everything—groceries, housing, and healthcare—will cost significantly more in the future. Here's how to stay ahead of rising costs:

- Invest in Inflation-Protected Bonds – Some investments, like Treasury Inflation-Protected Securities (TIPS), automatically increase in value as inflation rises, helping your money retain its buying power.

- Delay Social Security for Bigger Checks – If you wait until age 70 to claim Social Security, your monthly payment increases by 8% per year—ensuring you receive higher, guaranteed income later in life.

- Prepare for Higher Healthcare Costs – Medical expenses tend to increase faster than other costs. Consider:

- Long-term care insurance to cover nursing home or home care if needed.

- Health Savings Accounts (HSAs) to save tax-free for future medical expenses while you're still working.

Why Stay Financially Savvy in Retirement?

Financial stability is about more than just covering your bills—it gives you peace of mind and the freedom to enjoy life. Here's why staying financially aware matters:

- ☑ Supporting Your Desired Lifestyle – Financial security lets you travel, explore hobbies, volunteer, and spend time with loved ones, without financial stress.

☑ Handling Unexpected Expenses – Life happens. Health issues, home repairs, or inflation can derail your plans. A strong financial cushion helps manage surprises.

☑ Adapting to Modern Financial Solutions – Technology is making retirement finances easier than ever. Passive income, investment tools, and budgeting apps help retirees stay in control of their finances.

Final Thoughts: Making Your Money Work for You

Knowing where you stand financially is the first step to a secure retirement. But just as important is making sure your savings last as long as you do. By using smart withdrawal strategies, balancing investments, and protecting against inflation, you can enjoy financial freedom on your terms.

Ensuring your savings last is essential for retirement security. However, if your financial situation isn't as strong as you'd like, don't panic—there are proactive steps you can take. Let's explore whether delaying retirement or creating supplemental income could help bridge your financial gap.

If you're concerned your savings aren't sufficient or want added flexibility, the next section details how to easily create supplemental income without sacrificing your retirement freedom.

Delaying Retirement or Income Creation in Retirement

For some retirees, earning extra income is about staying engaged and pursuing passions. But for others, financial security may require a more structured approach—especially if savings aren't where they need to be.

Earlier in this chapter, we explored retirement savings benchmarks—such as the *10x final salary rule* and the *4% withdrawal rule*. If your savings don't align with these benchmarks or you're concerned about outliving your funds, delaying retirement or adding supplemental income could help bridge the gap and provide long-term financial stability.

Delaying Retirement or Income Creation in Retirement:
A Practical Strategy for Financial Stability

For those nearing retirement but feeling financially unprepared, delaying retirement even by a few years can be a powerful strategy.

- ✦ Delaying Social Security: Waiting until age 70 increases benefits by approximately 8% annually.
- ✦ Additional Savings & Investment Growth: Working longer allows more time to build savings and let investments grow.
- ✦ Bridging the Financial Gap: Even short-term, flexible income options can make a major difference in long-term financial stability.

How Do You Decide if You're Ready to Retire or Should Delay?

Retirement isn't just about reaching a certain age—it's about financial readiness, lifestyle goals, and personal circumstances. If you're wondering whether you should stay in the workforce a little longer or transition now, consider these key questions:

☑ **Do you have enough saved to sustain your desired lifestyle for 20-30 years?**
If your current savings require aggressive withdrawals to cover expenses, delaying retirement might allow you to save more, let investments grow, and reduce withdrawal rates later. Revisit the benchmarks we discussed earlier—if you're far below them, it may be worth considering a delay.

☑ **Are you financially flexible enough to handle unexpected costs?**
Consider whether you have an emergency fund and enough assets to cover rising healthcare costs, inflation, or market downturns without drastically adjusting your standard of living.

☑ **How does delaying affect your Social Security benefits?**
Delaying Social Security beyond full retirement age (67) can increase your monthly benefit by about 8% per year until age 70—giving you more guaranteed income for life.

☑ **Are you still engaged and fulfilled in your work?**
If you enjoy what you do and staying employed doesn't cause significant stress, working a few extra years can provide not only financial security but also social and mental benefits.

☑ **Have you explored part-time work or phased retirement?**
For those eager to step away from full-time work but not yet financially ready, a gradual transition through consulting, remote work, or a part-time role could provide additional income without giving up the flexibility of retirement.

If you answered 'no' to two or more of these, delaying retirement—even by just a couple of years—could significantly improve your long-term security.

In the next section, we'll explore how to create additional income in retirement—whether through consulting, passive income, or strategic investments. Because retirement isn't just about having enough—it's about creating financial confidence to live life on your terms.

But what does it take to position yourself for financial success in retirement? Just like in business, timing, strategy, and preparation make all the difference. Let's take a look at a real-world example of how being prepared at the right moment led to major financial opportunities—and how the same principles apply to retirement.

A Business Lesson in Timing, Strategy, and Financial Security

When it comes to financial security in retirement, timing and preparation matter just as much as they do in business. If you position yourself correctly, opportunities will come—but without a plan, you might find yourself scrambling for solutions instead.

I learned this firsthand in 2004. Our business was growing fast. We had hundreds of employees, an expanding market, and a clear vision for the future. But there was a challenge—to reach the next level, we needed a capital partner.

At first, we struggled. Two years earlier, we had pitched to investors, but they barely gave us the time of day. We were too small, too unknown, too risky. But instead of giving up, we kept building—strengthening our business, refining our strategy, and preparing for the moment when the right opportunity would come.

And then, the market shifted. Suddenly, our business was in high demand, and investors who had ignored us were now eager to get in. Within a single week, three private equity firms were at the table, offering valuations as high as $150 million for just half the company. The difference? We had positioned ourselves for success ahead of time, so when the opportunity arrived, we were ready.

The same principle applies to financial security in retirement. Just as businesses must prepare for the right moment, retirees must do the same. If you plan ahead, stay flexible, and build a strong financial foundation, you can seize opportunities rather than react to financial surprises.

We didn't just sit back and hope—we adapted, expanded, and positioned ourselves for future success. Retirement requires the same mindset. Whether it's adjusting your investments, identifying supplemental income sources, or ensuring your savings last, your ability to adapt will define your success.

Retirement isn't about taking reckless risks—it's about strategic decisions that give you options. When you approach your financial future with preparation and foresight, you're not just getting through retirement—you're thriving in it.

Whether you're investing in an interesting tech stock like NVIDIA or launching an online store, the principles stay the same: timing, strategy, and knowing when to act are key to building financial security. The same principles applied in my business experience, where preparation, adaptability, and smart decision-making led to significant financial opportunities.

This story isn't just a throwback to an interesting moment in my career—it's a reminder of the importance of setting a strong financial foundation, especially in retirement. Just like in business, retirement isn't about taking reckless risks—it's about positioning yourself for long-term financial success. While retirement might not be the time for aggressive investing or high-risk ventures, it is a time for smart, calculated moves based on sound due diligence.

Chapter 2 is about building that foundation—ensuring your resources work for you as part of a diversified retirement plan. With financial stability in place, you gain the freedom to pursue what truly excites you, all while feeling secure in your future.

Just as strategic planning and preparation opened doors in my business career, thoughtful financial planning in retirement opens opportunities for personal fulfillment. But beyond numbers and strategies, financial freedom means something different to everyone. Let me share what it meant for me.

What Does Financial Freedom Mean to You?

Take a moment to think about it. For some, financial freedom means having the peace of mind to cover unexpected expenses. For others, it's the ability to spend more time with family, travel, or explore new passions. But for me, it was something much deeper.

When I first retired, I thought I was financially prepared. I had planned for it. I had savings, investments, and a solid financial foundation. But what I didn't anticipate was how much of my identity was tied to my career. For years, my work had given me a sense of purpose—challenges to solve, goals to reach, and people to lead. Then, suddenly, it was all gone. I lost my passion, my drive, and my sense of direction.

I didn't realize how much I needed to reinvent myself in retirement. It wasn't just about financial security; it was about finding a new purpose—one that made me excited to wake up in the morning. That's when I turned to the Retirement Transition Framework (RTF).

Through the RTF, I mapped out what truly mattered to me beyond finances. I explored different ways to reignite my passion—writing, helping others, and staying engaged with new challenges. Eventually, I found a purpose that wasn't about making money but about making an impact. That became the new me in retirement.

So, what does financial freedom mean to you? It's more than just having enough in your bank account—it's about designing a retirement that aligns with your values, aspirations, and personal reinvention.

And while managing money is serious, retirement doesn't have to be. Whew, that was deep, so let's take a moment to lighten things up.

A Light Moment on Diversification

A retiree walks into a bank, sits down with the financial advisor, and says, "I need some help. I keep hearing everyone talk about 'diversifying my portfolio,' but I'm not even sure what that means."

The financial advisor smiles and responds, "Well, sir, it's simple. Imagine you have a basket full of eggs."

The retiree nods, and the advisor continues, "If all your eggs are in one basket, and you trip and fall, all your eggs will break. But if you spread them out across multiple baskets, even if one basket drops, you'll still have eggs in the other baskets."

The retiree pauses, thinking deeply, then says, "I see... So, what you're saying is, I need more eggs."

While financial stability gives you peace of mind, many retirees find that having a little extra income—whether out of necessity or passion—adds another layer of security and purpose. And the good news? Earning in retirement doesn't have to mean going back to a 9-to-5 grind.

Thanks to technology, the internet, and changing work trends, it's easier than ever to generate income on your own terms—from anywhere. While financial stability provides peace of mind, many retirees find that earning a little extra—whether to cover rising costs or pursue a passion—adds both security and purpose.

Creating Supplemental Income in Retirement Without a Full-Time Job

Many retirees find that earning a little extra—whether to cover rising costs or pursue a passion—adds both security and purpose. But here's the good news: earning in retirement no longer means going back to a 9-to-5 job.

Today's technology and work trends offer more ways than ever to generate income on your own terms. Whether it's part-time consulting, turning a hobby into a side business, or creating passive income streams, retirees now have flexible options to supplement their income without sacrificing freedom.

Now, let's explore some of the best ways to leverage your skills, interests, and assets to generate income in retirement.

Here are some examples to consider:

1. Part-Time Work and Consulting:

Many retirees find fulfillment in working part-time, whether in their previous field or a completely new role. Part-time work provides both income and social engagement while allowing for flexibility.

- ✦ Consulting or Freelancing: Leverage decades of experience by offering services on platforms like Upwork or Fiverr.
- ✦ Teaching or Coaching: Retired educators and professionals can mentor, coach, or teach online courses via platforms like Udemy or Teachable.

2. Leveraging the Internet for Income

The digital economy has opened countless opportunities to generate income from home.

- ✦ Sell Handmade Crafts or Digital Products: Use platforms like Etsy or Gumroad to sell handmade goods, eBooks, or printables.
- ✦ Monetize a Blog or YouTube Channel: Retirees passionate about travel, fitness, or hobbies can create content that generates ad revenue and affiliate commissions.
- ✦ Rent Out a Spare Room: Platforms like Airbnb or VRBO allow retirees to turn unused space into income without long-term commitments.

3. Investing in Income-Generating Assets

For those who prefer a passive income, investing in income-producing assets can provide steady cash flow in retirement.

- ✦ Real Estate Rentals: Owning rental properties or investing in Real Estate Investment Trusts (REITs) can create additional revenue streams.

- Fixed Annuities: A guaranteed source of income that provides financial security without market volatility.

Understanding Income vs. Passive Income

To build financial stability, it's important to distinguish between active income (which requires continuous effort) and passive income (which provides earnings with minimal ongoing work).

Have you ever thought about what it would be like to earn money while sipping coffee at home?

- Passive Income involves setting up income streams—such as dividends, rental properties, or royalties—that require minimal ongoing effort, though some may need occasional oversight.

- Active Income, like consulting or freelancing, stops as soon as you stop working.

A balanced mix of both active and passive income provides financial stability and flexibility, allowing you to enjoy retirement on your own terms.

Note: Passive income doesn't mean zero effort—it means setting up systems that generate income with minimal ongoing involvement. Some sources, like dividends and annuities, require almost no work, while others, like rental properties or digital businesses, require occasional management. The key is choosing sources that align with your desired level of engagement and financial goals. For example, see the chart below summarizing key factors to consider by category:

Business Activity Comparison Table

Business Activity	Labor Content	Delegatability	Portability (Travel-Friendly)	Capital Requirement	Technology Requirement	Reliability
Consulting/Freelancing	High	Low	High	Low	Medium	Medium
Teaching Online Courses	Medium	Medium	High	Low	High	High
Selling Digital Products	Low	High	High	Low	High	High
Affiliate Marketing	Low	High	High	Low	Medium	Medium
Real Estate Rentals	Medium	Medium	Medium	High	Low	High
Dropshipping	Low	High	High	Low	High	Medium
Stock Dividends	None	N/A	High	High	Low	High
YouTube/Blog Monetization	Medium	High	High	Low	High	Medium
Subscription-Based Content	Medium	High	High	Low	Medium	Medium
Airbnb Hosting	Medium	Medium	Low	Medium	Medium	Medium
Franchise Ownership	High	Low	Low	High	Low	Medium
E-commerce Store	High	Medium	Medium	Medium	High	Medium

Identifying Your Income Gap – Using Technology for Supplemental Income in Retirement

For many retirees, the goal isn't launching a full-fledged business—it's ensuring financial security while maintaining flexibility. Whether it's covering an income shortfall, managing unexpected expenses, or funding new interests, technology has made it easier than ever to generate income without a full-time job.

Before exploring income opportunities, consider:

1. Do you have an income gap that needs addressing?
2. Are you seeking a financial cushion to manage rising costs like healthcare?
3. Or do you just want to turn a hobby into a rewarding side income?

Once you identify your needs, the next step is choosing low-risk, flexible, and technology-driven income solutions that fit your lifestyle.

Top Technology-Driven Ways to Generate Supplemental Income

1. AI-Powered Tools – Earning Without the Heavy Lifting

Artificial Intelligence (AI) allows retirees to generate income with minimal effort by automating tasks.

+ Automating customer service: AI chatbots handle client inquiries without manual work.
+ Creating digital content: AI-powered writing and design tools can help create online courses or eBooks.
+ Marketing automation: AI-driven ad platforms optimize income for those selling products or services.

Example: A retired consultant could create an AI-assisted online coaching program that runs itself.

2. Digital Products & Online Courses – Sharing Knowledge for Passive Income

✦ Platforms like Udemy, Teachable, and Gumroad allow retirees to package their expertise into digital products with minimal ongoing effort.

Example: A retired accountant could create an online course on retirement tax strategies for passive income.

3. The Digital Economy – Selling Without Physical Inventory

✦ Print-on-Demand & Dropshipping: Platforms like Shopify, WooCommerce, and Amazon FBA let retirees sell custom products without handling inventory.

Example: A retiree with a passion for design can sell custom t-shirts or digital art prints using print-on-demand services.

4. Affiliate Marketing – Earning from Recommendations

✦ Recommend products and earn commissions on sales made through your unique referral links.

Example: A retiree who writes a travel blog can earn commissions by recommending travel gear or retirement-friendly destinations.

5. Subscription-Based Models – Turning Hobbies into Recurring Income

✦ Platforms like Substack and Patreon allow retirees to monetize their expertise or hobbies through a paid membership model.

Example: A retired educator could launch a monthly newsletter on lifelong learning for paying subscribers.

Key Takeaway: Income as a Financial Safety Net, Not a Full-Time Job

Technology has removed many barriers to earning income in retirement. Whether your goal is to fill a financial gap, build a safety cushion, or fund new interests, today's asset-light, low-risk options provide the flexibility to earn on your own terms.

By identifying your income needs first, you can select the right opportunities to maintain financial stability without sacrificing your freedom.

Budgeting in retirement is different. It's no longer about saving for someday—it *is* someday. Suddenly, you're calculating whether your grandkid's birthday gift should come with batteries *included* or *suggested*.

And those free afternoons? They're great… until you realize "free time" and "free money" are not the same thing.

Action Plan for Achieving Financial Stability in Retirement

1. Assess Your Financial Landscape

Step: Conduct a comprehensive review of your current financial situation. Make a list of all your assets, liabilities, income sources, and monthly expenses. Don't just stop at the basics; consider things like future healthcare costs, potential inheritances, and even inflation's impact over time.

Goal: Complete this assessment by month-end, ideally with the guidance of a financial advisor who specializes in retirement.

2. Analyze and Optimize Your Investments

Step: Examine your portfolio with a fine-toothed comb. Are you adequately diversified? How are you positioned across different asset classes? Are you overexposed to risk? Balancing your portfolio between high-yield bonds, dividend stocks, and low-risk assets is crucial. Additionally, consider the tax implications of your investments and any opportunities to minimize your tax burden.

Goal: Rebalance your portfolio annually, adjusting for market changes and shifts in your risk tolerance as you age.

3. Maximize Income-Generating Opportunities

Step: Identify a mix of active and passive income opportunities that suit your skills and interests. For active income, consider consulting or freelancing. For passive income, investigate REITs, dividend-paying stocks, or peer-to-peer lending platforms. The goal is to have a diversified income stream that doesn't rely solely on one source.

Goal: Within the next three months, add at least one new income stream to your portfolio. Test the waters with a small investment or a single client to gauge your interest and the income potential.

4. Create a Retirement Budget and Stick to It

Step: Develop a comprehensive budget that accounts for fixed and discretionary spending. Use online budgeting tools or apps to track your spending and ensure you're living within your means. Remember to allocate funds for leisure activities, travel, and emergencies.

Goal: Set a budget within the next month and revisit it quarterly. Adjust based on changes in income, expenses, and your overall financial goals.

5. Implement Regular Financial Check-Ins

Step: Schedule regular reviews of your financial situation. Look at how your income streams are performing, evaluate the returns on your investments, and reassess your goals. Staying informed will allow you to make quick adjustments in response to market changes or personal circumstances.

Goal: Commit to quarterly financial check-ins to ensure alignment with your long-term objectives and adjust as needed.

Action Plan Summary

Step	What to Do	Goal (When)
1	**Assess Financial Landscape** (assets, debts, income, expenses, future costs)	Complete detailed financial assessment by end of this month
2	**Analyze & Optimize Investments** (diversification, risk levels, tax implications)	Annual portfolio rebalance
3	**Maximize Income Opportunities** (identify suitable active/passive income streams)	Add one new income source within 3 months
4	**Create & Maintain Retirement Budget** (include leisure, emergencies, discretionary spending)	Set initial budget within 1 month; quarterly adjustments
5	**Regular Financial Check-Ins** (review income, investments, adjust plans accordingly)	Quarterly financial check-ins

Where to Get Professional Guidance:

While this chapter provides strategies to strengthen your financial foundation, every retiree's situation is unique. A financial professional can help tailor these strategies to your specific needs. Here are some resources to consider:

- ✦ **Certified Financial Planners (CFP®)** – Help with retirement planning, investments, and tax-efficient withdrawal strategies.

- ✦ **Retirement Income Specialists** – Focus on maximizing Social Security, annuities, and passive income sources.

- ✦ **Estate Planning Attorneys** – Assist with wills, trusts, and legacy planning.

- ✦ **Tax Advisors** – Help minimize taxes on withdrawals, Social Security, and investments.

Uplifting Case Studies: Retirees Navigating Financial Challenges and Opportunities

There's probably never been a better time to create passive income than today, thanks to modern technology. With various digital platforms and apps, you can build an income stream without leaving your house, often with minimal upfront investment. Let's look at how some retirees are using these tools to create fulfilling and flexible ways to make money.

1. Marianne's Consulting Journey

After retiring, Marianne missed daily interactions and decided to leverage her HR expertise part-time. She now consults remotely with small businesses on HR policies using WebEx.

Key Takeaways:

+ Leverage existing expertise into part-time work.
+ Remote technology (WebEx) enables flexibility.
+ Supplemental income complements the retirement lifestyle without sacrificing freedom or personal interests.

2. John's Airbnb Adventure

When John's children moved out, he transformed empty bedrooms into Airbnb rentals, managing everything effortlessly from his smartphone or laptop. The income supports travel and lifestyle, with technology simplifying guest management.

Key Takeaways:

+ Turn unused home space into income.
+ Smartphone apps automate bookings, payments, and guest interactions.
+ Passive income funds lifestyle without tapping savings.

3. Helen's Part-Time Passion

Facing concerns about retirement funds, Helen turned her passion for gardening into an Etsy shop selling plants and supplies. She expanded by offering gardening workshops on Zoom, creating both income and community connections.

Key Takeaways:

- ✦ Monetize personal interests through online marketplaces (Etsy).
- ✦ Leverage video conferencing (Zoom) to expand reach.
- ✦ Enjoyable side income boosts finances and fulfillment.

4. Jack's Rental Venture

Jack converted his vacation home into short-term rentals listed on Airbnb and Vrbo. Using automation tools like Hostfully, he manages bookings remotely, generating consistent income with minimal hands-on work.

Key Takeaways:

- ✦ Utilize assets (vacation home) to generate rental income.
- ✦ Automation (Hostfully) reduces workload, increases flexibility.
- ✦ Reliable passive income creates financial stability.

5. Maria's Online Store

Maria, a retired jewelry designer, relaunched her craft through online stores on Shopify and Etsy. Integrated inventory management and social media marketing attract customers, generating automated sales and passive income.

Key Takeaways:

- ✦ Restart previous skills/hobbies via e-commerce (Shopify, Etsy).
- ✦ Automated sales systems reduce workload.
- ✦ Social media marketing drives continuous sales with minimal effort.

Final Thoughts: Embracing Financial Security as a Path to Fulfillment

Start by assessing where you stand financially and what adjustments you can make now to create the retirement you deserve. Managing your finances in retirement is about more than just making ends meet; it's about creating a stable foundation that supports a fulfilling and purpose-driven life. By staying proactive and exploring new ways to generate income, you can enjoy the freedom to pursue what matters most to you.

Now, take 10 minutes to jot down where you stand today—your savings, income streams, and any financial gaps. This will be your first step toward building a retirement on your terms. Because retirement isn't just about money—it's about the life you design with it.

Chapter 2 Takeaways: Financial Stability Is Your Launchpad

☑ **Retirement readiness is a widespread concern.**
Nearly half of retirees have less than $100,000 saved, and only 25% feel financially secure. Financial stress can derail even the best-laid retirement plans.

☑ **Financial stability isn't just about money—it's about resilience.**
From inflation to divorce, life throws curveballs. A solid financial foundation helps you adapt, pivot, and move forward with confidence.

☑ **Supplemental income can be a safety net or a passion project.**
Thanks to technology and new work trends, retirees can earn without going back to a full-time job. Passive income, consulting, and digital tools offer flexible options.

☑ **Preparation creates opportunity.**
Like in business, timing and readiness in retirement matter. Those who prepare early are in the best position to thrive, not just survive.

☑ **The Retirement Transition Framework (RTF) starts with financial security.**
Without it, purpose, identity, and reinvention become much harder to access. Money doesn't buy happiness, but it creates the freedom to find it.

For years, I thought financial success was the answer to a fulfilling retirement. But after stepping away from my career, I learned the hard way that money alone wasn't enough. What I needed—what we all need—is a deeper sense of purpose. Many retirees struggle with financial readiness, but an even bigger challenge awaits—what comes next when the work stops? Money is crucial, but meaning is just as essential. In Chapter 3, we'll uncover how to bridge that gap.

Important Note: This Book is Not Financial Advice

The information in this book is for educational purposes only and should not be considered financial, tax, or legal advice. Every individual's financial situation is different, and the strategies discussed here may not be suitable for your unique circumstances. Always consult a qualified financial professional before making investment, retirement, or tax decisions.

Retirement's Dirty Little Secret: Why Purpose Matters As Much As Money

📍 **What you will learn:** Financial security is your foundation. Without it, everything else in retirement is harder to build.

"The purpose of life is not to be happy. It is to be useful, to be honorable, to be compassionate... to have it make some difference that you have lived and lived well."
— *Ralph Waldo Emerson*

Let's Revisit a Hard Truth

We touched on this in the introduction, but it deserves a deeper look here, because it's not just my story. It's a reality shared by millions. Many retirees, even those who are financially secure, still feel a surprising sense of loss, disconnection, or restlessness. In this chapter, we'll unpack why that happens, what the research reveals, and how the Retirement Transition Framework (RTF) can help you find clarity, purpose, and momentum in this new chapter of life.

When "Freedom" Isn't Enough: Why Retirees Still Feel Lost

By now, you've probably seen the glossy version of retirement: golf, pickleball, travel, naps, beach walks, dinner with friends. I certainly did. But after the initial high of "freedom," I found myself staring at a full calendar... and still feeling empty.

One morning, I glanced at our week—bike ride, Netflix, drinks with friends, and said to Suzanne, "We're booked solid this week... doing absolutely nothing productive." It was a wake-up call. I didn't miss the meetings or pressure, but I missed contributing. I missed doing something that mattered.

Here's the truth: many retirees who've done everything "right" financially still feel a surprising sense of loss, disconnection, or restlessness. It's not talked about often— maybe because it's personal or even a little embarrassing—but it's real, and more common than most people think.

In fact, studies show that financial freedom alone doesn't guarantee emotional fulfillment. For many, it leads to a lingering question: *Now what?*

As Dr. Barbara B. Levin puts it:

"Work doesn't just provide income; it offers social connections, structure, and a sense of contribution."

When Even Tom Brady Feels Lost

Legendary quarterback Tom Brady once put it bluntly:

"You can't stop chasing purpose. The moment you do, you start dying."

He's not wrong. After retiring twice, he admitted that life without football left a real void.

"When I'm not playing football, I'm like, 'Who am I?'" he said.

That's the emotional side of retirement that people don't talk about enough—the sudden loss of built-in purpose. Even the most successful people feel it. Brady's not talking about touchdowns here—he's talking about identity.

Maybe that's why he went back to playing after his first retirement. When something defines you for decades, walking away isn't just a career move—it's an identity crisis.

This chapter picks up where Chapter 1 left off. You've faced those same questions. Now let's figure out what to do with them.

Beyond the Numbers: What Comes After the Planning?

You've likely spent years getting your financial ducks in a row—saving, budgeting, running the numbers. But here's the curveball: even with all that in place, many retirees still find themselves asking, *"Now what?"*

Because once the checks stop and the calendar opens up, what you're really left with isn't just free time—it's the space to figure out what still gives your life energy, purpose, and meaning.

And for others, the question hits differently: *"What if I'm not financially 'done,' but I still want to live with intention?"*

This is where the Retirement Transition Framework (RTF) comes in. Financial stability is just the first step. The deeper challenge—and the greater opportunity—is crafting a life of purpose, fulfillment, and forward momentum.

The Hidden Gift of Work: Understanding What Gave You Meaning

Before diving into how to build a fulfilling retirement, take a moment to reflect: What was it about work that gave you a sense of meaning? It's easy to assume that work was just a source of income, but for many, it also provided something deeper—a sense of purpose, structure, and connection that is hard to replace overnight.

Tony Robbins articulates this idea well:

"There are six basic human needs that every single person on the planet tries to fulfill: Certainty, variety, connection, growth, contribution, and significance."

When you think about it, work often meets many of these needs:

- ✦ Certainty – A steady paycheck, a routine, knowing what to expect each day.
- ✦ Variety – Facing new challenges, solving problems, and engaging with different people.
- ✦ Connection – Friendships, teamwork, feeling part of something bigger.
- ✦ Growth – Learning new skills, progressing in your career.
- ✦ Contribution – Feeling that your work made a difference in the world.
- ✦ Significance – Being valued, respected, and recognized for your efforts.

Now that work is behind you, which of these needs are still being met? And more importantly, which ones feel missing?

Many retirees struggle because they haven't identified what they need to replace or reinvent in retirement. If work provided a sense of contribution, how can you still make an impact? If it provided growth, how can you continue learning? If it gave you structure, how can you create a new daily rhythm?

By taking stock of what truly fulfilled you in your working years, you can begin designing a retirement that feels just as meaningful—without the need for a paycheck.

A Personal Journey

That process of reflection led me to some surprising places.

A few months into retirement, Suzanne and I were in New York City when a close friend helped arrange a private meeting with Megyn Kelly, a former network news anchor and now a leading podcast news host. Suzanne had read Megyn's book and found striking parallels between her own journey and Megyn's story. The meeting was more for Suzanne than for me—but witnessing her excitement made the moment special for both of us. (And let's be honest—Megyn's charisma didn't exactly hurt the experience for me.)

We met Megyn in her dressing room—just the three of us—and talked about everything from careers and kids to politics and reinvention. Whether or not you agree with her public views, she was incredibly warm, down-to-earth, and thoughtful. Later, without us asking, she sent Suzanne a signed copy of her book with a personal note. It was a small gesture, but it meant a lot.

That experience reminded me of something I had lost in the day-to-day quiet of early retirement: the joy of meaningful conversation, connection, and curiosity. Even without a career, I still had things to learn, to offer, and to share.

That realization helped me start shifting my thinking from what I had walked away from, to what I still wanted to step into.

The Search for Purpose

In this chapter, we'll explore the hidden challenges retirees often face when financial security is achieved but emotional fulfillment feels out of reach. Retirement can create a profound sense of disconnection when the structure and identity tied to work disappear. Yet, there's good news: the transition to a fulfilling retirement is within your control. We'll explore how you can move beyond financial security and step into a new phase filled with meaning, curiosity, and renewed purpose.

The Leap Into the Unknown

It's like the skydiving scene in *The Bucket List*. Edward is calm and collected; Carter is petrified. That leap from the plane isn't just about adrenaline—it's about surrendering control and trusting you'll land on your feet.

Retirement feels a lot like that.

You leave behind the security of your role, the rhythm of your calendar, the familiar sense of being needed. And suddenly, you're in free fall. No titles. No deadlines. No urgent emails. Just wide-open space and the unnerving question: *Now what?*

At first, that freedom can feel disorienting. The silence is louder than expected. The days stretch longer. You realize that, for decades, your identity wasn't just about what you did—it was *who* you were.

But here's the shift: just like Carter in that skydive, once you stop fighting the fall, something surprising happens. You look around, and instead of fear, you feel possibility. This is your chance to reinvent—not retire. To let go of outdated definitions and create something on your terms.

You're not falling. You're *flying*—if you're willing to change how you see it.

From Uncertainty to Action: Tools to Reclaim Your Purpose

Up to this point, we've talked about the emotional challenges that can surface after retirement—loss of identity, lack of structure, and the question of purpose. But here's the shift: you're not stuck. In fact, you're now in the perfect position to rebuild your next chapter with clarity, freedom, and meaning.

This next section introduces practical tools and frameworks—ones that have helped countless retirees turn their uncertainty into direction. These aren't abstract ideas. They're actionable, research-backed models to help you rewrite the script.

The Good News: You Can Rewrite the Script

In fact, despite the daunting statistics, here's the good news: you are not defined by your job title. And while the initial transition might feel overwhelming, it also offers the opportunity to find purpose on your terms. Research shows that retirees who actively seek new roles, hobbies, or challenges experience a significant increase in life satisfaction. In fact, a study conducted by the National Institute on Aging found that 30% of retirees successfully navigate retirement by discovering joy in new activities like volunteer work, travel, or creative pursuits. This group of retirees finds retirement not to be a time of loss but a chance to redefine success and meaning.

Contrasting Views: A Framework for Reinvention

Many retirees find that retirement gives them the time and space to pursue passions that once felt unreachable. Dr. William Bridges, in his book *Transitions*, provides a framework for managing major life changes in three phases:

1. An ending (letting go of your past identity),

2. The neutral zone (a time of reflection and figuring things out), and

3. A new beginning (embracing a new purpose).

Bridges encourages retirees to use the neutral zone to explore their values, dreams, and aspirations—reframing retirement as a time for growth, not just relaxation.

Applying Bridges' Framework: A Real-Life Example

Let's imagine Carol, a former CEO who spent over 30 years climbing the corporate ladder. When she retired, she felt an initial sense of freedom—but that quickly gave way to feeling unsettled. After so many years tied to her role, she no longer knew who she was without it and spent months grappling with the question: *"Who am I now?"*

In the neutral zone, she began reflecting on her interests outside of work, like photography and environmental activism. It wasn't easy at first—she spent much of this time feeling uncertain and uncomfortable, but this phase was critical. By allowing herself the space to reflect without pressure, she started reconnecting with the things she enjoyed before her career took over.

Finally, in the new beginning phase, Carol found her purpose by merging her love for photography with her passion for environmental issues. She started volunteering with an environmental non-profit, using her photography skills to help raise awareness for conservation efforts. In doing so, she found a new sense of identity, one that was rooted in personal passion rather than professional success.

This example shows how the three phases of Bridges' framework provide an easy to follow path for retirees to reinvent themselves and embrace new purpose.

Expanding the HERO Model for Finding Purpose

Another powerful framework is the HERO model, developed by Dr. Richard J. Leider in his book *The Power of Purpose*. According to Leider, there are four key elements to a fulfilling retirement:

1. **H = Hope:** Envision a future filled with possibility. What do you want your post-career life to look like? Having a hopeful outlook increases resilience and motivation.

   Example: Mark, a retired engineer, felt stuck when he retired, but he began envisioning a future where he could combine his technical skills with his love of teaching. This vision gave him the hope and drive to pursue tutoring students in engineering, rekindling a sense of purpose.

2. **E = Efficacy:** Believe in your ability to make a difference. Whether it's through volunteering, mentorship, or spending more time with loved ones, remind yourself that your actions still matter.

   Example: Sarah, a former sales manager, struggled to find meaning after retirement until she started mentoring young entrepreneurs. Her decades of experience suddenly became a valuable resource, and she rediscovered her sense of contribution.

3. **R = Resilience:** Accept that setbacks and challenges are part of the journey. Retirement is a time of transition, and with it comes uncertainty. Building resilience means bouncing back from setbacks and staying focused on what brings you joy and fulfillment, even when things don't go as planned.

   Example: Tom faced health issues soon after retiring, which limited his ability to pursue his hobbies. Instead of becoming discouraged, he learned new skills like painting and photography—activities that matched his physical capabilities and gave him new ways to express his creativity.

4. **O = Openness:** Embrace curiosity and be open to new experiences. Retirement gives you the freedom to explore, experiment, and try things you never had time for before.

Example: Joan, a lifelong customer service representative, never had time to explore her interest in music. In retirement, she took up piano lessons, an activity she had always wanted to try. Embracing this new hobby gave her a fresh sense of excitement and joy.

Discovering the Missing Piece: Purpose Beyond Work

Imagine this: You've spent decades dreaming about retirement—the freedom from early alarms, meetings, and endless deadlines. You finally have the chance to live without the constraints of work. But after the initial excitement fades, you might start to feel that something's missing. Days stretch out, and without the structure of work, your sense of identity and purpose may waver.

This feeling is more common than you think. Retirement is not just about leisure and relaxation; it's a psychological and emotional transformation. What gives your life meaning now? What gets you out of bed in the morning?

Retirement Isn't One Thing — It's a System

One of the most valuable lessons I picked up in business school was something called the *Complementary Assets Model*, developed by David Teece. It was originally designed for innovation strategy—but when I applied it to retirement, it made more sense than anything else I'd read.

The core idea is simple: an invention only creates real value when it's supported by the right system around it. You can invent a car, but without roads, gas stations, traffic laws, and mechanics, it's not all that useful. Same goes for a smartphone—without Wi-Fi, apps, and power, it's just an expensive paperweight.

The same thing applies to retirement.

On paper, retirement sounds ideal. No more meetings. No early alarms. Freedom to do what you want. But without the right surrounding elements—things like purpose, health, financial stability, relationships, and a reason to get out of bed in the morning—it can fall flat. What looks like freedom can start to feel like floating. For me, it wasn't just floating—it felt more like drifting in space without a tether. No mission. No gravity. Just me, my calendar, and a lot of time to overthink things...

usually in sweatpants! Eventually, I realized the problem wasn't a lack of free time—it was a lack of fulfillment. And to get that back, I had to build something more intentional. That's when I started seeing retirement for what it really is: a system. And fulfillment, I found, comes from putting the right complementary assets in place—*each of which aligns with the Retirement Transition Framework you'll see throughout this book.*

Here's what that might look like:

Innovation	Complementary Assets
Retirement	*Purpose, Health, Finances, Community, Curiosity, Faith, Lifelong Learning*

These are your *retirement infrastructure*—your *complementary assets*. Just like a car needs roads, gas, and a license to be useful, retirement needs more than money to be fulfilling. The more complementary assets you build around your retirement, the stronger and more fulfilling your system becomes.

It's not about having everything figured out on day one. It's about intentionally creating the system that supports the life you want to live.

We'll come back to this idea again in Chapter 9 when we talk about staying current with technology. That's where this model really comes alive in practical ways. But for now, just remember retirement isn't one thing—it's a system. And the great part? You get to build it.

Action Plan: Finding Purpose Beyond Financial Planning

As you move beyond financial security and into discovering your new purpose in retirement, here are five actionable steps you can take:

1. **Reflect on What Excites You:**
    + Ask yourself: *What gives me joy? What activities make me feel alive?* Whether it's a hobby, social engagement, or learning something new, begin by identifying the activities that spark excitement in your life.

✦ Remember to think about this as a clean slate. You have this amazing opportunity to start fresh and focus on what, as my mom used to say, "makes your tail wag."

2. **Reframe Your Identity:**

✦ Let go of the notion that your identity is tied to your career. Start focusing on who you are outside of work by listing your values, passions, and strengths. This will help you embrace a new sense of self rooted in personal fulfillment.

✦ *I would not have said this a year ago, but forget your past work and how that defined you. Create a new identity that has passion and purpose that means something to you. I went from a risk management executive to an author and Disaster Action Team specialist at the Red Cross.*

3. **Engage in a New Role:**

✦ Explore volunteer opportunities, mentoring, or starting a project that aligns with your interests. Small steps, like joining a local group or offering your expertise in a new setting, can provide meaning and structure.

✦ Trial and error are part of the process. I took several volunteer roles that just didn't fit for me until I ultimately found the right ones with organizations focused on helping people and animals.

4. **Apply the HERO Model:**

✦ Use Dr. Richard Leider's HERO model to guide your journey:

  ◆ **H**ope: Envision a positive future.

  ◆ **E**fficacy: Believe in your ability to make a difference.

  ◆ **R**esilience: Embrace setbacks and keep moving forward.

  ◆ **O**penness: Stay curious and open to new experiences.

✦ Models can sometimes feel too academic, but if you really try and use this model the way it's described earlier in the chapter, it works. It did for me anyway.

5. **Find Your Flow:**
   - ✦ Identify activities where you can get fully absorbed and lose track of time, such as creative hobbies, learning new skills, or even pursuing fitness goals. Activities that put you in a flow state can greatly enhance your sense of purpose and well-being.

I was never a writer—unless you count the thousands of quick emails and texts I cranked out over the years. But something shifted in retirement. When I started writing this book, I noticed something strange—in the best way. I'd sit down to write, and suddenly three hours had passed. I wasn't watching the clock. I was just in it. That's a "flow state." It's what happens when your brain locks in, and time seems to disappear. It's not just productive—it's deeply fulfilling. You'll know you've found your version of it when something grabs your attention so fully that you lose track of everything else. That's when you know you're getting close to your purpose.

Final Thoughts: Retirement as a New Beginning

Retirement represents a powerful new beginning—an opportunity to redefine success and purpose on your own terms. You've now seen that having a strong financial plan is just the start. The real work—and the real growth—comes from rediscovering who you are when the job title disappears.

But knowing that purpose matters is only the beginning. The next challenge is often the hardest: embracing the discomfort of change.

Change isn't linear. It's messy, emotional, and at times overwhelming. Whether you're grieving the end of your career or excited to begin something new, you're not alone in this space of in-between. That's why the next step in the Retirement Transition Framework (RTF) is all about learning how to let go of what was and step forward with courage and clarity.

Chapter 3 Takeaways: *When Financial Freedom Isn't Enough*

- ☑ **Retirement can still feel empty—even when you're financially prepared.**
  Emotional fulfillment isn't guaranteed by a strong portfolio.

- ☑ **Your identity may be more tied to your work than you realize.**
  Letting go of a professional role often triggers disconnection and restlessness.

- ☑ **Purpose isn't optional—it's essential.**
  As Tom Brady put it: *"You can't stop chasing purpose. The moment you do, you start dying."*

- ☑ **The Retirement Transition Framework (RTF) helps you move forward.**
  Use proven models like the Bridges Transition Framework and HERO Model to redefine identity and direction.

- ☑ **Retirement is a system—not a single decision.**
  Like a car needs roads and gas to be useful, retirement needs complementary assets: purpose, health, relationships, curiosity, and more.

In Chapter 4: *Embracing Change – Moving Forward with Confidence*, we'll explore what it really takes to move through this emotional transition and start living life on your terms again.

Before you turn the page, take 5 minutes to jot down: What makes your tail wag?

Adapting to Change – Moving Forward with Confidence

🖈 **What you will learn:** Change is uncomfortable, but it's the path forward. Adapting with intention leads to growth.

"Change is hard at first, messy in the middle, and gorgeous at the end."
— *Robin Sharma*

What If Adapting to Change Was the Key to Reinvention?

Picture this: after decades of hard work, meetings, and deadlines, you finally reach retirement. It feels like a reward for all those years of effort. But then a question pops up: *What now?* How do you redefine yourself after leaving behind a career that shaped so much of your life?

Retirement, as it turns out, is not just about slowing down. It's about reinvention. This is a time to transition into something new—a version of you that isn't tied to your career but is focused on personal fulfillment, curiosity, and connection. The freedom you've gained isn't just a break from work; it's a chance to take control of your next chapter and build a new sense of identity and purpose.

In this chapter, we'll explore how to actively approach this new phase, shedding old identities, navigating challenges, and finding confidence in the unknown. This represents a key step in the Retirement Transition Framework (RTF): letting go. Before you can move forward with purpose, you must release the identity that once defined you.

Now that we've made the case for finding purpose in retirement, the first step is to *take control* of this new chapter, rather than letting the difficulties that come with it hold you back. I resisted at first, which delayed my journey toward discovering a new sense of purpose and identity. But once I shifted my mindset and actively engaged in the process, everything started to change.

Redefining Retirement: From Status to Fulfillment

As we touched on in Chapter 3, retirement today isn't just about slowing down—it's about reinvention. We're living longer, staying healthier, and being presented with more tools than ever to build a meaningful second act.

It's no longer just a "winding down" period. More retirees are learning new skills, exploring creative outlets, engaging in their communities, and even launching passion-driven ventures. The paycheck may no longer be essential—but purpose still is.

And here's the deeper shift: success isn't measured by your title anymore. It's measured by how fulfilled you feel, how connected you are, and how curious you remain. That's the version of success that truly matters now—and it's one you get to define.

Letting Go of Your Professional Identity: The Emotional Rollercoaster

Here's the truth: letting go of your professional identity is tough. For years, work has given you structure, meaning, and maybe even a sense of importance, so it's only natural to feel a bit lost when you step away from that. Many retirees describe it as standing at the edge of an unfamiliar landscape—everything you've known about yourself tied to your job starts to shift. It's a confusing, sometimes disorienting feeling. And that's okay.

My Own Experience with Letting Go

I remember vividly how hard it was for me to step away from my professional identity. I spent years as a strategist, an idea guy, an owner. I worked in large companies, transitioned to smaller ones, then moved into startups. My last gig was with a small company we eventually sold. You'd think scaling down from massive corporate environments to more hands-on roles would've made the transition easier—but it didn't. I went from the high-pressure grind of board meetings and shareholder updates to a less intense startup pace, yet the shift into retirement still left me feeling disconnected.

Startups are, of course, incredibly hard and demanding, but with fewer people and less bureaucratic machinery, it's a different type of pressure. I figured that scaling down before retiring would help me transition smoothly, but it didn't. Even though my last position wasn't under the hot light of constant interrogation found in big companies, the transition to retirement still left me feeling disconnected.

That feeling of emptiness took me by surprise. I wasn't expecting to feel so adrift after retirement. But what I realized was that my career, as rewarding as it was, had kept me from exploring other parts of who I am. For years, my time, energy, and even my sense of self had been consumed by the work I did. Now that I had the freedom to explore new sides of myself, I didn't know where to start. But that freedom—after some reflection—eventually became a gift.

The Turning Point

For a long time, I held onto my professional identity, clinging to the idea that I had to maintain relevance through work. But one day, it hit me: I had the opportunity to *redefine success on my terms*. No deadlines, no board meetings, no teams to manage—just me, and the things that I found meaningful. I could *choose* who I wanted to be next.

"I'm evolving away from tennis, toward other things that are important to me."
— Serena Williams

Serena didn't say she was retiring—she said she was evolving. That shift in mindset embodies the heart of this chapter: you're not quitting; you're growing into something new. Serena transitioned into family, business, and activism with grace and focus—and that same mindset works beautifully in retirement.

That same approach works in retirement. You're not stepping down—you're stepping into.

I learned early on in my career that you sometimes need to roll with unexpected situations and embrace the humor in them.

The Bread Roll Incident: A Lesson in Adaptability

You might be surprised how often adaptability—and a little humility—comes in handy.

Years ago, I was at a dinner interview for a sales job with two gentlemen. Everything was going smoothly until the waiter brought over a basket of bread, placing a roll on each of our plates. One of the interviewers asked me a question, and in my eagerness to look confident and passionate, I went for a big hand gesture to make my point.

As I swung my hand forward, back angled like a 9-iron, I made perfect contact with the roll, sending it flying across the restaurant in a soaring arc. And here's the kicker:

it was *way* better than I've ever hit a golf shot on an actual course. I mean, dead center, full carry, no slice—pure magic. Just... not the kind of magic you want at a job interview.

I froze. The interviewer got up, walked calmly across the room, picked up the runaway roll, and placed it silently back on my plate. Nobody said a word. Somehow, I still got the job.

Looking back, that moment taught me more than I realized. Life—just like that interview—is full of surprises, misfires, and awkward moments. But it's how you recover, stay grounded, and keep moving forward that matters.

In retirement, those same principles apply. Things won't always go smoothly. You'll try new things that might flop, feel uncomfortable, or embarrass yourself in new ways. But just like that flying bread roll, you'll survive—and probably laugh about it later. Letting go of control and embracing imperfection? That's where the real freedom starts.

Adapting Through Humor and Humility

Exploring new hobbies and tackling life's curveballs isn't just about staying busy — it's a way to keep your mind sharp and your outlook fresh. When we stretch beyond our comfort zones, even in small or humorous ways, we build the emotional muscle needed to adapt. Moments like the infamous bread roll incident remind us: adaptability isn't about being flawless — it's about staying flexible and being able to laugh at yourself along the way.

That shift in perspective was a game changer for me. I began to realize that I wasn't just a retired executive anymore — I was someone with the freedom to pursue interests I had long set aside. I could finally explore creativity, deepen relationships that once took a backseat to career, and rediscover parts of myself that had been on pause for decades.

Of course, it wasn't all smooth sailing. Leaving behind a role that had defined me for years brought a surprising wave of emotions — grief, anxiety, even fear. I didn't expect that. Like many, I assumed retirement would be a smooth glide into the next chapter. But those feelings weren't signs of weakness. They were signs of transition — and proof that something inside me was shifting.

When I first stepped away from my career and started volunteering, I assumed it would be a natural extension of the life I had built — a chance to stay useful and give back. I figured my experience would translate seamlessly and that meaning would follow. But on my very first day, I was assigned to give tours at a nursing home — and I came home more depressed than I had ever felt in my working life. Rather than feeling helpful, I felt like I was staring into my future.

I couldn't explain it at the time. On paper, everything looked right: I had financial stability, my health, and a good amount of free time. But emotionally, I was spiraling — quietly, and without a name for what I was going through.

Later, I came across something called the Kübler-Ross Transition Curve. Originally developed to describe the five stages of grief, it has since been widely adopted to explain how we emotionally process change, including retirement. This visual highlights the emotional stages—denial, anger, bargaining, depression, and acceptance—often encountered during this process.

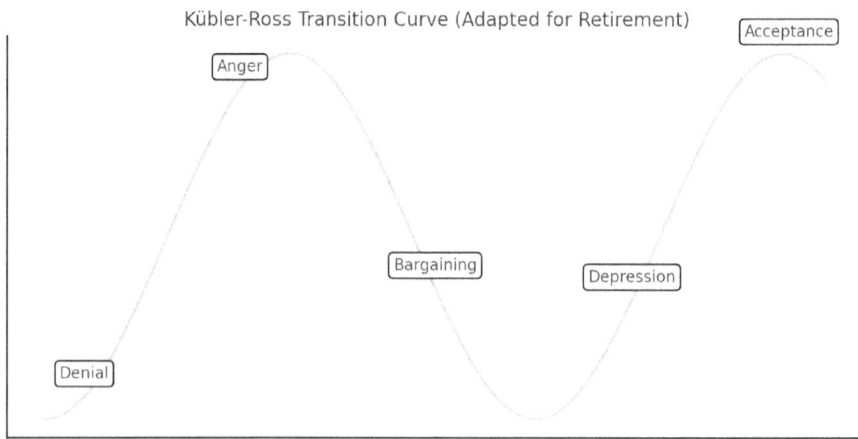

Let's be honest: few of us expect to *grieve* retirement. Isn't this supposed to be a victory lap? But here's the truth — you can experience every one of those stages, even when you've done everything right.

- ✦ Denial: "This isn't retirement — it's just a break."

- ✦ Anger: "Why do I feel invisible all of a sudden?"

- ✦ Bargaining: "Maybe I should start consulting... just to feel useful again."

- ✦ Depression: "Is this really all there is now?"

- ✦ Acceptance: "I get it. I need to build a new life — not recreate the old one."

Looking back, it took humility to admit I wasn't immune. And it took humor to get through it — like when I showed up to my first volunteer shift with a clipboard and binder, and someone asked if I was there from the health department. I had to laugh at myself. That moment helped me realize this was something new — not a continuation of my past, but the beginning of something entirely different.

That's when I started building again — with intention this time. What pulled me out of that low point wasn't just time. It was structure, purpose, and a clear plan. That's what ultimately led to the creation of the Retirement Transition Framework (RTF) — a flexible, practical system to help navigate this new phase with purpose. Letting go of my former identity wasn't easy—but it had to come first. In the RTF, this is the foundational step: releasing the past so you can fully embrace what's next. It helped me move beyond my lost identity and toward the life I was meant to create.

Here's the encouraging part: the bottom of that curve? It isn't a failure. It's the launchpad. If you find yourself down there — confused, frustrated, unsure — don't panic. That's not the end of your story. It's the beginning of your reinvention.

Your Identity Doesn't Live in a Cubicle

Remember that iconic scene in *Office Space* where Peter finally stops caring about his soul-crushing job? He knocks down his cubicle walls, ignores his boss, and strolls into the office with a carefree attitude. It's a humorous take on what it feels like to stop letting your work define you. Peter essentially flips the switch from being chained to his job to fully embracing the freedom that comes with letting go.

Now, I'm not suggesting you grab a sledgehammer and start tearing down cubicles, although let's be honest, that does sound kind of fun! What I'm saying is, much like Peter, you don't need to let your corporate life dictate your happiness. Letting go of that professional identity can be a freeing experience.

The deeper point here is that Peter's happiness wasn't tied to his job title or the work he did. Once he shed the weight of his corporate identity, he found a new sense of freedom. And that's the kind of freedom many retirees experience when they finally release the pressure of their careers. You realize your value doesn't come from the title you held or the work you did—it's in the person you are and the choices you make moving forward. It's about embracing the idea that this new chapter is yours to shape however you see fit.

Why Letting Go Matters: A Psychologist's Perspective

Dr. Susan Whitbourne, a psychologist who studies life transitions, explains that stepping away from a career can trigger feelings of loss and uncertainty. "Letting go doesn't mean forgetting who you were," she says. "It means making space for who you're becoming."

It's a powerful idea. Stepping into this new chapter isn't about abandoning everything that made you successful. It's about evolving those strengths into new opportunities. You still carry all that experience, all those skills—but now you get to apply them in ways that are more aligned with what brings you joy and fulfillment.

Research: Identity's Role in Well-Being

Letting go of your career is about more than "moving on." Research shows that retirees who find new roles and hobbies report higher life satisfaction and better emotional health. Dr. Carol Ryff, a researcher on well-being, explains, "Retirement is an opportunity to redefine what success and purpose look like on your terms."

This insight underscores the fact that retirement isn't just a transition from a job—it's an opportunity to reshape your entire outlook on life. By letting go of the professional identity you once held, you open the door to explore new roles and experiences that can enrich your retirement journey.

New Story: Rick's Rediscovery of Creativity

Let me tell you about Rick. For 35 years, Rick worked as an engineer, designing bridges and infrastructure projects. His work was technical, precise, and respected. But after retirement, Rick found himself feeling disconnected. Without the daily structure and the clear goals his career provided, he felt uncertain about how to spend his time.

Then one day, Rick's granddaughter asked him to help her build a treehouse in the backyard. At first, Rick was hesitant—he hadn't built something like that in years. But as he started drawing plans and gathering materials, he rediscovered a passion for hands-on work. Building that treehouse became more than just a project; it reignited Rick's love for creative problem-solving and craftsmanship.

That treehouse turned into something much bigger for Rick. It reminded him that the skills he had built over decades didn't disappear with retirement. He just needed to reframe them. Rick went on to volunteer with a local community center, helping them design and build playgrounds. He found a new sense of purpose by adapting to change and reimagining how he could use the strengths he had spent years developing.

Metaphor: Letting Go to Make Room for the New

Think of your career as an old couch. It's been comfortable and familiar, sticking with you through all of life's ups and downs. But over time, it becomes a bit worn out and no longer serves its purpose. Still, parting with it is hard. We cling to old roles and identities out of comfort, habit, and maybe even fear.

But here's the thing—just like you eventually need to replace that old couch, clinging to outdated identities can keep you from moving forward. Holding onto a past version of yourself blocks the way for something new and exciting to enter your life.

🔎 Deep Dive Exercise: The Letting Go Practice

Letting go of your old identity isn't just a mental shift—it's about taking deliberate, concrete steps toward a more purpose-driven chapter of life. Use this four-step framework to guide the transition:

Step 1: Analyze Past Successes

Action: Reflect on three specific moments in your career when you felt most successful, fulfilled, or deeply engaged.

Task: Identify the strengths or traits that made those moments possible. These are part of who you are, not just your job.

Example: If mentoring a team member was a highlight, your core strength might be *guidance or teaching*. This could translate into mentoring, volunteering, or even coaching in retirement.

Step 2: Acknowledge What You're Losing—and What You're Gaining

Action: Write down what's hardest to let go of—whether it's structure, status, or being the go-to person.

Task: For each item, list a corresponding benefit of releasing it.

Example: If you're letting go of your workday structure, the upside might be the freedom to build your own rhythm. No more alarms, no more Monday dread.

Step 3: Reframe Your Core Strengths

Action: Revisit the strengths from Step 1. These qualities didn't retire when you did.

Task: List two ways each strength could apply to your life now—through hobbies, community service, creative pursuits, or mentoring.

Example: If your strength was problem-solving, could you apply that to help a local nonprofit, or consult with startups needing operational insight?

Step 4: Set Clear Goals for Your Next Chapter

Action: Visualize your ideal life one year from now. How do you want to feel? What do you want to be doing?

Task: Set three specific, measurable goals tied to your vision. Keep them achievable, with timelines.

Examples:

- ✦ Enroll in a class within 30 days.
- ✦ Join a local group or club by next week.
- ✦ Create a weekly schedule for volunteering, hobbies, or physical wellness.

✷ **Bonus Tip: Make It Stick**

Let's be honest—some people love journaling. I'm not one of them. I've tried, but I usually stare at the page like it owes me money.

Instead, I started texting myself ideas or leaving voice memos—usually while at the dog park, in the grocery store, or mid-workout. Not exactly glamorous, but hey, the best ideas show up when your hands are full or you're sweaty. Later, I'd scroll through those random notes and think, *"Huh, that's actually a decent thought,"* and work it into my plans. It became one of the most useful habits I picked up while writing this book.

You don't need a fancy system—just find what works for you and do it consistently. If journaling helps, great. If it's sticky notes, a notes app, or scribbles on a napkin, that works too. The goal is to capture the sparks when they fly and turn them into something real.

Bonus points if you actually follow through and put it on a calendar. Turning those ideas into specific actions and setting a few reminders (that you don't ignore) can make all the difference.

Because this isn't just about reflecting—it's about re-engaging. You're not only letting go of who you were, you're actively building what's next. And that deserves more than a passing thought—it deserves a plan. Or at least a voice memo with enthusiasm.

Conclusion: Letting Go Is a Process, Not a One-Time Event

This isn't about dwelling on the past—it's about creating momentum for the future. Every step brings you closer to the new version of yourself, one that's grounded in who you are now and where you're heading. By taking deliberate actions, you open the door to growth, learning, and self-discovery.

Letting go is a process that unfolds over time, not something that happens in a single moment. You might revisit these exercises multiple times as you adjust to new roles and challenges in your retirement journey. And that's okay—each revisit allows for deeper reflection and growth. Remember, you're not erasing your past accomplishments; you're simply evolving, applying your strengths in new ways that align with your current stage of life.

Chapter 4 Takeaways:
Letting Go to Move Forward

✅ **Letting go of your professional identity is emotional—but essential.**
You're not losing who you were. You're making room for who you're becoming.

✅ **Retirement is less about endings and more about reinvention.**
Change can feel uncomfortable, but it's also the path to growth, freedom, and new purpose.

✅ **Grieving your old role is normal.**
Using tools like the Kübler-Ross Transition Curve can help you process emotions and embrace the next chapter with clarity.

✅ **Adaptability and humility are your retirement superpowers.**
Whether it's volunteering misfires or flying bread rolls, learning to laugh at the awkward moments is key to moving forward.

✅ **You still carry your strengths—now you get to reapply them.**
By reframing what made you great at work, you can channel those skills into passions, creativity, or service in retirement.

✅ **This step of the Retirement Transition Framework (RTF) is about release.**
To fully step into who you want to become, you have to stop clinging to who you used to be.

Next Step: Chapter 5 – Redefining Success: Achieving Fulfillment in Retirement

Now that you've taken this step in the Retirement Transition Framework (RTF)—letting go of your professional identity—it's time to move forward. In Chapter 5, *Redefining Success: Achieving Fulfillment in Retirement*, we'll shift the focus from career-based accomplishments to personal fulfillment. This is where real growth begins—where you move beyond what you did for a living and start embracing who you are and what brings you joy. We'll explore how to use the RTF to guide this transition and help you define success on your terms. With the past behind you, the path ahead is yours to shape.

Redefining Success – Achieving Fulfillment in Retirement

🍶 **What you will learn:** Success in retirement isn't about achievements but alignment with what truly matters to you.

"Don't aim for success if you want it; just do what you love and believe in, and it will come naturally."
— *David Frost*

Discovering New Horizons

Imagine this: after decades of building a career, checking off goals, and collecting achievements, you step into retirement. The old markers of success—titles, promotions, financial milestones—start to fade, much like trophies gathering dust. But here's the exciting part: a whole new horizon is waiting, one defined by fulfillment through personal satisfaction, meaningful relationships, and lifelong learning. This chapter represents the next step in the Retirement Transition Framework (RTF): Redefining Success. In this phase, the focus shifts from external achievements to discovering what brings internal fulfillment, purpose, and joy.

Shifting the Focus: Redefining Success on Your Terms

Success in retirement isn't about titles or promotions anymore—you've been there, done that. Now, it's about discovering what brings you alive. As Tony Robbins puts it, "Success without fulfillment is the ultimate failure." This phase of life offers a golden opportunity to rediscover passions you may have set aside while focusing on your career.

Take Lisa, for example. A former marketing executive, she always loved nature but never had the time to nurture it. In retirement, she transformed her backyard into a vibrant garden filled with vegetables, native plants, and butterfly habitats. She started documenting her journey on social media, connecting with other retirees and even local schools. For Lisa, success wasn't about output—it was about growth, beauty, and sharing something meaningful with others.

"We're not meant to be static creatures. We're meant to keep growing."
— *Jane Fonda*

Fonda's continual reinvention—into her 80s—proves that growth doesn't stop when the paycheck does. She challenges the narrative that aging means slowing down. For her, success in later life is defined by relevance, advocacy, and ongoing engagement.

From Career to Camaraderie: Finding Connection Beyond Titles

(Note: The names in the following story have been changed to protect the individual's privacy. Their accomplishments and roles remain accurately represented.)

Letting go of a career doesn't mean letting go of ambition, connection, or a sense of humor. It's about embracing what comes next and continuing to find meaning, sometimes in unexpected ways. Even the most accomplished individuals seek out new challenges, and they certainly don't leave their sense of camaraderie behind.

This brings to mind a moment from a board meeting where I was asked to present an update on my division's performance. I wasn't a board member, but the board I was presenting to was no ordinary one. Seated around the table were some of the most distinguished leaders I had ever met: Colonel Jack Hayes, a former Apollo mission commander, and decorated Air Force pilot; Mr. Keith Langford, a billionaire entrepreneur, prominent philanthropist, and co-founder of a Fortune 100 retail empire; and Mr. Robert Marks, fellow co-founder of that same company and a visionary in his own right. These were just three members of an exceptionally accomplished board—each person around the table brought a unique legacy of leadership, innovation, and impact. It was surreal to be in the same room, presenting my results to such high-profile figures.

Colonel Hayes arrived late to the meeting, still wearing his flight suit. He had flown a military jet into Atlanta and, rather than change into business attire, came straight to the meeting. Langford looked over and, with a grin, said, "What the hell, Jack? You couldn't even change your clothes? You wore your pajamas to a board meeting?" Hayes just scowled at him in return—classic no-nonsense astronaut energy.

About ninety minutes into the meeting, Hayes suddenly stood up and said he had to leave. Langford, a bit surprised, asked, "What, already?" Without missing a beat, Hayes replied, "I've got to get the jet back—I don't have a freakin' private jet like you." (Though I'm cleaning up the F-word he actually used.) The room burst into laughter.

It was one of those moments that reminded me that no matter how accomplished or well-known someone is, they still act like regular guys when they're busting each other's chops. Watching these titans of space and business trade jabs was not only hilarious—it was grounding. It reminded me that, in the end, we're all just people—human, humble, and wired for connection.

That moment stuck with me—not just because it was funny, but because it showed that the importance of camaraderie, laughter, and shared experiences doesn't fade after retirement. It's what makes life, well, fun.

Expert Insights: Understanding the Psychology of Fulfillment

Dr. Richard Rohr, in his book *Falling Upward*, describes the second half of life as a time to shift from external achievements to internal significance. He argues that this phase is not about adding to your life but discovering the deeper meaning that's already there. It's about tapping into the joy that comes from aligning your actions with your values and passions.

Dr. Mihaly Csikszentmihalyi (now that's a last name!) is known for his groundbreaking work on the concept of "flow." According to Csikszentmihalyi, fulfillment often comes from deep engagement in activities that challenge us and absorb our attention. In his book *Flow: The Psychology of Optimal Experience*, he explains that people are happiest when they are fully immersed in activities that require skill and create a sense of mastery.

This "flow state" is when you lose track of time because you're so absorbed in what you're doing. It's that feeling of being so deeply involved in an activity that everything else fades into the background. You've probably experienced it at some point, whether it was during a work project, a creative pursuit, or even playing a sport.

Expanding on Flow: Why It Matters

In retirement, finding fulfillment often comes from discovering and nurturing moments of *flow*—a state where you're so immersed in an activity that time seems to stand still. Psychologist Dr. Mihaly Csikszentmihalyi, in his book *Flow: The Psychology of Optimal Experience*, defines it as the sweet spot where your skills perfectly match the challenge, creating deep focus and enjoyment.

Think back to a time when hours flew by because you were fully engaged—maybe writing, painting, building something, or playing a sport. That's flow. It's not just fun—it's one of the keys to happiness and mental well-being.

In retirement, flow replaces the structure work once provided. It helps you stay mentally sharp, emotionally fulfilled, and connected to a sense of purpose.

Why Flow is Key to Retirement Fulfillment

Achieving flow is more than just an enjoyable experience. Csikszentmihalyi's research shows that people who regularly experience flow are happier, more fulfilled, and even enjoy improved mental and emotional well-being. In retirement, flow can help replace the structure that a career once provided, offering you the mental and emotional engagement necessary to thrive.

For example, when I sit down to write, I often lose track of time because I'm so absorbed in the process. What feels like 15 minutes can turn into three hours. That's flow in action. It's a clear sign that I've found an activity that challenges and excites me in a deeply rewarding way. This level of engagement isn't just about productivity—it's about finding joy in the process, not just the outcome.

How to Create Flow in Your Retirement

The good news is that retirement offers a unique opportunity to explore activities that can help you achieve this sense of flow. Without the distractions and demands of a career, you can dive into creative pursuits, physical activities, or intellectual challenges that genuinely excite and engage you. Whether it's woodworking, gardening, writing, or learning a new skill like photography, these activities give you the opportunity to experience flow and, in turn, deeper fulfillment.

By tapping into what brings you into a flow state, you create a retirement that's not just about relaxation but about meaningful engagement in the things you care about. Whether it's starting a community project, picking up an old hobby, or challenging yourself to master a new skill, these moments of flow can redefine your sense of success and purpose in this next phase of life.

Rediscovering Old Passions: A New Source of Fulfillment

Sometimes, fulfillment in retirement isn't about reinventing the wheel—it's about rediscovering what once lit you up. Author Steven Pressfield, in his book *The War of Art*, emphasizes how many of us abandon our creative passions because of the demands of life, only to rediscover them when we have the time and space. Retirement offers that time, making it the perfect opportunity to dust off old hobbies and pursuits.

Jeri's Rediscovery of Woodworking

Take Jeri, for example. She was a dedicated R.N. who envisioned retirement as a well-earned chance to finally relax and take it easy. But after a few months, she found herself restless and uninspired. That's when she remembered her passion for woodworking, a hobby she had enjoyed in her younger years but never had time to pursue seriously.

She cleared out her garage, dusted off her old tools, and started building again. With the help of YouTube tutorials and woodworking communities on Reddit, Jeri quickly sharpened her skills. What began as a way to pass the time turned into a full-blown passion. These days, she crafts furniture and donates her pieces to local charities, combining creativity with service—something that's always been part of who she is.

For Jeri, retirement wasn't about stepping away from meaning—it was about finding it in new, unexpected ways that made her feel fully alive.

John's Rediscovery of Art

Similarly, John, a retired sales executive, stumbled upon his old set of paints while cleaning out the attic. On a whim, he signed up for online courses on Skillshare and dove headfirst into painting. Before long, he was showcasing his work at local art fairs—and even selling a few pieces. For John, painting wasn't just a hobby; it became a creative outlet and a way to connect with others. Online communities kept him motivated and inspired.

Both Jeri and John show us that retirement isn't about fading into the background. It's a time to reignite the passions you once loved—or to discover new ones you never had time for before.

Rick's Rediscovery of Creativity

And then there's Rick. For 35 years, Rick worked as an engineer, designing bridges and infrastructure. His work was technical, precise, and respected. But after retiring, Rick felt unmoored. Without the clear goals and structured routine of his career, he wasn't sure how to spend his time—or even who he was without his job.

Then one day, Rick's granddaughter asked him to help build a treehouse in the backyard. At first, he hesitated—he hadn't done anything like that in years. But as he started sketching plans and gathering materials, something clicked. The project brought back his love for hands-on problem-solving and craftsmanship. He lost track of time working on it, fully engaged and, for the first time in a while, deeply fulfilled.

That treehouse sparked something in Rick. He began volunteering with a local community center, using his engineering and design skills to help build playgrounds. What started as a small moment with his granddaughter became a launchpad for rediscovering a core part of himself, reminding him that his strengths didn't retire when he did.

Building Meaningful Connections: The True Wealth of Retirement

One of the most significant shifts in retirement is moving from transactional relationships—those focused on work and productivity—to deeper, more meaningful ones. Author Brené Brown writes in *Daring Greatly* that *"Connection is why we're here; it is what gives purpose and meaning to our lives."* In retirement, the opportunity to strengthen connections with loved ones, friends, and even new acquaintances is invaluable.

Research: Social Bonds and Well-Being

Dr. Julianne Holt-Lunstad's research shows that strong social connections can increase life expectancy, boost mental health, and improve overall well-being. In fact, the effects of social isolation are as harmful as smoking 15 cigarettes a day. And yet, many retirees face the challenge of staying connected, especially after leaving the workplace.

The good news is that technology makes it easier to maintain those connections. Whether it's joining a virtual book club, hopping into a fitness class on Zoom, or simply reconnecting with old friends over WhatsApp, staying socially engaged is more accessible than ever. Facebook Groups, Meetup, and Eventbrite offer countless ways to meet new people and keep your social calendar full.

Elaine's Potluck Tradition

I can't believe I'm actually talking about a Potluck, but hey, it's true and relevant. No judgments, please, and don't tell Suzanne! Take Elaine, a retired project manager. She knew the importance of staying social, so she started hosting monthly potlucks with her friends. When they couldn't meet in person, they kept the tradition alive through virtual dinners on Zoom. Elaine's story is a reminder that while retirement might change how we connect, it doesn't have to end our social lives. Whether in person or online, staying connected is one of the most fulfilling aspects of this phase.

Mental Health and Growth: Staying Engaged in Retirement

Just as your body needs exercise, so does your brain. Lifelong learning is a key to staying sharp and emotionally resilient in retirement. Dr. Norman Doidge, in his book *The Brain That Changes Itself*, explains how the brain remains plastic throughout life, meaning it can form new neural pathways even in old age. Learning new skills, whether it's a language, a craft, or a subject you've always been curious about, keeps your mind active and engaged.

Brian's Cognitive Boost Through Language Learning

Take Brian, a retired warehouse supervisor. He decided to learn Italian using Duolingo and reinforced his progress by watching Italian films on Netflix—part learning, part entertainment. Not only did his memory improve, but he also felt more mentally alert and engaged. Platforms like Babbel and Rosetta Stone offer fun, accessible ways to keep your brain buzzing, while Coursera and edX provide a gateway to university-level courses without ever leaving your couch.

Sarah's Emotional Resilience

Building emotional resilience is key to thriving in retirement. Sarah, a retired teacher, struggled with the loss of structure in her daily life. She joined an art therapy group through Meetup, which helped her process her emotions and build new friendships. Platforms like BetterHelp and Talkspace offer virtual therapy sessions, making it easier than ever to prioritize emotional wellness.

The Freedom of Letting Go: A Movie Scene for Inspiration

Remember the scene in *Dead Poets Society* where Robin Williams' character, Mr. Keating, urges his students to *"seize the day"*? The boys stand on their desks and shout, *"Oh Captain! My Captain!"* as they embrace the idea of living life with passion and purpose, beyond societal expectations. This moment is a perfect metaphor for retirement.

In the same way, retirement invites you to stand up, let go of the limiting beliefs that come with your old job title, and embrace a new purpose. It's your time to *"seize the day"* and redefine success on your terms.

Your Passion Quest: A 30-Day Action Plan

I know the idea of finding new passions in retirement can seem daunting at first. Trust me, I've been there. But if we break it down into small, actionable steps, the process can be fun and even fulfilling. I had to pull out my old psychology degree for this one! It might sound a bit esoteric at first, but you know by now that I speak in plain, simple sentences. So, let's keep it real. This 30-day action plan is designed to help you explore, experiment, and discover what truly excites you in this next chapter.

1. **Discovery Day:** Explore multiple activities that spark curiosity and interest.
2. **30-Day Passion Project:** Choose one activity to dive into for a month.
3. **Passion Mapping:** Reflect, identify patterns, and map future directions.
4. **Stay Open:** Continue exploring, stay curious, and adapt over time.

Here's how to approach it:

1. The Discovery Day: A Full Day of Exploration

The first step in your passion quest is setting aside one day to immerse yourself in activities that spark curiosity and inspiration. Think of it like a "choose your own adventure" day, where you just let yourself explore what pulls at your interest. The goal is to have fun with it, without pressure.

Ideas for Discovery Day:

- ✦ **Visit a Museum or Gallery:** If art intrigues you but life got in the way, spend the day admiring pieces you never had time for. Bring a notebook and jot down what catches your eye.

- ✦ **Take a Cooking Class:** Ever thought about channeling your inner chef? Cooking classes, whether local or online, are a fun way to test the waters and discover if cooking might be your next passion. Suzanne and I went to a couple of cooking classes in Europe, and it really upped the ante! If you travel, try this wherever you go. And, if you visit the U.S., don't miss the deep-dish pizza at Giordano's in Chicago—it's not a cooking class, but it's a must-try!

- ✦ **Nature Walks:** Take a walk in the park, or better yet, explore a nature reserve. Let the tranquility of nature wash over you and see if that connection feels right. I do this a little differently by taking our dogs, Beaux and Bowser, to different parks for that nature-feel experience.

- ✦ **Watch Documentaries:** Ever want to learn about something entirely new? Pick a subject and binge-watch documentaries. Let your curiosity guide you—maybe it's space exploration or ancient civilizations. I'm a big fan of documentaries and movies based on true stories. Sometimes real life is just unbelievable—or funny enough!

- ✦ **Try a Workshop:** You could sign up for anything—photography, pottery, woodworking. Hands-on experience is often where you really feel out whether something might stick.

- ✦ **Explore Technology:** If gadgets and technology spark your curiosity, check out online courses in areas like graphic design or even coding. You might find something you never thought you'd enjoy. I must admit I'm an early adopter of technology. I love trying the newest phones, AI (this one even makes images to poke fun at my friends), and electric cars!

Reflection: At the end of the day, jot down some notes. What left you feeling excited? What didn't? Think about why certain activities stood out and how they made you feel. No pressure, just some casual self-reflection.

2. The 30-Day Passion Project: Dive Deep Into One Activity

Once you've completed your Discovery Day, pick one activity that intrigued or excited you. This is what you'll focus on for the next 30 days. Now, I'm not saying you need to go full throttle—just commit to exploring this interest a little bit every day. The goal is to really immerse yourself and see if that initial spark turns into a flame.

Commit to Growth:

- ✦ **Learn a New Skill:** Whether it's playing the guitar, perfecting a new recipe, or learning a language, give it a go. Set small goals to keep the momentum going. Even baby steps lead to progress.

- ✦ **Volunteer:** If giving back resonates with you, find a cause and commit to helping regularly. It doesn't have to be a big commitment—just enough to see if it adds meaning to your days.

- ✦ **Creative Arts:** If painting or writing got your attention, give yourself time to explore it daily. Don't worry about being perfect—it's all about the process.

- ✦ **Physical Wellness:** If staying active is your thing, get creative. Maybe it's yoga, hiking, or dance. Make time for it regularly and see how your body and mind respond. I'll jump in on this one and recommend the occasional blood test to track something you want to focus on. You don't need to see your doctor for this anymore—both Quest Diagnostics and LabCorp offer consumer sites to explore and order tests. Of course, this isn't a replacement for your regular doctor visits!

Journaling and Progress Tracking: Throughout the 30 days, some people find journaling effective, but it's not really my thing. Instead, what worked for me was setting reminders or texting myself whenever I had a thought. Whether at the dog park, in the store, or even during a workout, I'd send myself a quick note so I could come back to it later. Honestly, it was super helpful for keeping track of ideas and moments of inspiration.

Adapting Along the Way: Don't be afraid to switch gears if something isn't quite working for you. There's no failure here—just discovery. If an activity feels like a chore rather than a joy, feel free to pivot. Life's too short not to enjoy what you're doing!

3. Passion Mapping: Uncover Patterns and Opportunities

After 30 days, it's time to step back and reflect on your experiences. This is where things start to click. Look at the activities you loved and the ones that didn't hit the mark. Here's how to process it all:

Reflection Questions:

- ✦ **What sparked joy?** Go back to your notes or texts. What kept you engaged and excited?
- ✦ **What felt challenging but rewarding?** Sometimes the best passions are the ones that push you just enough. Did you feel that way with any of your projects?
- ✦ **What didn't resonate?** Not everything will be a hit. Be honest about what didn't work and why.

Creating a Passion Map: Now, here's where it gets fun. Create a map—whether on paper or using an app like MindMeister—that links your enjoyable activities to potential future paths. If woodworking brought you joy, maybe you want to turn that into a regular hobby or even a side business. If volunteering felt fulfilling, explore how you can make a bigger impact in that area. It's all about connecting the dots to build a future that excites you.

4. **Bonus Tip: Stay Open to New Possibilities**

Remember, passions can change. What excites you today may evolve or lead to new interests down the line, and that's perfectly normal. The key is staying open to trying new things and seeing where they take you. Keep exploring, keep learning, and keep growing. The beauty of this phase of life is that you finally have the freedom to pursue what lights you up.

Conclusion: Redefining Success in Retirement

Success in retirement isn't about letting go of your past accomplishments—it's about creating new ones. The key is personal fulfillment, building meaningful social connections, and staying mentally engaged. Technology plays a supporting role, but the heart of success lies in growth, connection, and discovery.

This is your time to embrace new opportunities, rediscover old passions, and design the retirement you've always dreamed of. This chapter completes the second step in the Retirement Transition Framework (RTF): Redefining Success. You've begun shifting from career-centered achievements to a more personal and purpose-driven definition of success—one that's rooted in who you are now and what you value most.

Chapter 5 Takeaways: Redefining Success – Achieving Fulfillment in Retirement

RTF Step 3: Redefining Success & Finding Fulfillment

- ☑ Success in retirement is about personal fulfillment, not career achievements.
- ☑ Reignite old passions or discover new ones—personal growth doesn't stop at retirement.
- ☑ Build meaningful relationships and deepen connections with family, friends, and community.
- ☑ Stay mentally sharp and emotionally engaged through lifelong learning and activities that challenge your brain.
- ☑ Use technology as a tool but remember—it's the human experience that creates lasting fulfillment.

✸ What's Next in the RTF Journey?

You've now completed Step 3 in the Retirement Transition Framework.

Next up: **Chapter 6 – Exploring New Passions: Turning Curiosity into Purpose**. We'll dive into how to identify and cultivate interests that light you up—and how to keep them alive through lifelong learning, volunteering, and meaningful engagement with your community. It's time to turn curiosity into a fulfilling and purpose-driven retirement.

Exploring New Passions – Turning Curiosity into Purpose

📍 **What you will learn:** Purpose doesn't arrive fully formed—
it starts with curiosity and grows through action.

*"Don't ask what the world needs. Ask what makes you
come alive and go do it. Because what the world needs is
people who have come alive"*
— *Howard Thurman*

What If You've Been Preparing for This All Wrong?

You've probably heard it before: "Retirement is the golden era." But as you learned in a previous chapter, only 27% of retirees report feeling truly fulfilled, according to the *Journal of Aging Studies*. That means nearly three-quarters of retirees are left thinking, *Is this it?*

Why? Because most of us were handed the wrong map for navigating this stage of life. We've been led to believe retirement is about "winding down" or "taking it easy." But let's be real: does that sound like the path to satisfaction? For most people, it doesn't even come close.

So, what if the real key to enjoying this time isn't slowing down but igniting a whole new fire? This chapter is about flipping the retirement script, turning curiosity into your North Star, and discovering fresh adventures that keep you engaged and fulfilled—on your terms. We're leaving the old, stale roadmap behind and embracing a model where curiosity, creativity, and connection drive us forward.

For years, I had my hands full with work and family, often daydreaming about the "someday" when I'd have time to dive into my personal interests. But when that day arrived, I was shocked by an unexpected feeling—I didn't even know where to start! All the things I'd once been curious about seemed distant, and I realized that 'someday' had finally come, but my map was outdated. Exploring those curiosities wasn't just an option; it turned out to be essential for filling my days with purpose, joy, and a sense of adventure.

Get ready to throw out the cliché images of shuffleboard and "senior discounts" (unless that's your thing). We're diving into the real journey: a retirement that's more like your second act, one where you get to explore who you really are and what lights you up.

This chapter aligns with Step 4 of the Retirement Transition Framework (RTF): Exploring New Passions and Purpose.

In this chapter, we'll explore how curiosity can lead to a deeper sense of purpose, and we'll provide actionable steps to help you transform your passions into a fulfilling new identity. You'll also learn how to stay mentally sharp and emotionally engaged, all while having fun.

For me, the emptiness of having nothing to strive for or challenge me was overwhelming. It wasn't just that I felt lazy or unproductive—it was the realization that life had suddenly become stagnant, devoid of excitement or purpose. Sure, the best part of retirement seemed to be the freedom to do whatever I wanted, whenever I wanted, and I kept myself busy with just that. I used to joke, 'We're super busy doing absolutely nothing productive,' and at the time, it was funny—and maybe even a little enjoyable. But deep down, I knew something was off. Without purpose, retirement felt like it was slowly draining the life out of me. I thought, 'Freedom is great, but retirement? Without something to drive me, it sucks.'

Turning Curiosity into Purpose

Now that we've looked at fulfillment beyond career achievements, let's dive into how curiosity can lead to a deeper sense of purpose in retirement. This chapter is about reconnecting with old hobbies or diving into brand-new interests that spark joy and personal growth.

Real-Life Transformations Through Passion

Carlos's Story – Curiosity Turned into a New Calling

Carlos spent 35 years as a postal worker. He had never seen himself as particularly creative, but he always had a quiet curiosity about baking bread. Retirement gave him the time and mental space to try something new. What started as a few loaves of sourdough from YouTube tutorials turned into a weekly ritual. He began giving fresh-baked loaves to neighbors, then teaching a small class at the local community center. For Carlos, baking wasn't just a hobby—it became a way to share warmth and community, one loaf at a time.

It's funny how curiosity can show up in the quietest corners—or the loudest rooms.

💡 A Lighter Take: Mike Tyson, McGregor, and Embracing the Unexpected

You never know where curiosity—or spontaneous engagement—might lead. One of the most unexpected moments for me? Meeting Mike Tyson the day after the Mayweather-McGregor crossover fight...

It happened to be the day after Conor McGregor fought Floyd Mayweather Jr. in that wild boxing/UFC crossover match.

After being introduced to Mike, I just blurted out, *"So... thoughts on the McGregor fight?"*

Mike nodded and said, *"Better than I thought he'd do."*

Without thinking, I joked, *"Yeah, I was waiting for McGregor to forget he was boxing and just throw a roundhouse kick to Mayweather's head and end it."*

That's when Mike's eyes lit up and he leaned in, saying, *"Hell yes—or grab him from behind and put him dark!"* And to really sell it, he motioned like he was putting me in a rear chokehold.

I looked at him and said, *"Ok, Mike... now you're kinda scaring me."*

He laughed and said, *"Sorry! Ha ha."*

I survived. Barely. But more importantly, I walked away with one of the most unexpectedly hilarious encounters of my life—and a reminder that keeping things light, playful, and spontaneous is one of the best ways to stay mentally engaged in this next phase of life.

Embracing Curiosity and New Experiences

Whether it's an old pastime or a fresh interest, embracing your curiosity keeps the mind active, enriches your days, and may even lead to unexpected friendships. You can explore virtually any interest with technology's help—from cooking classes and nature photography to travel planning and online learning communities. This journey of exploration is about tapping into your curiosity and letting it guide you to new, enriching experiences.

Here's why this matters: Passion isn't just something to keep you busy; it's a core part of feeling fulfilled in retirement. Discovering new interests or reigniting old ones can transform this stage of life, helping you to replace that sense of purpose you once felt in your career with something deeply satisfying. Think of it as a way to reconnect with what brings you joy, curiosity, and even a bit of adventure. For me, passion in any stage of life is critical. I understand it will not always be a job or a family, but everyone needs to be fulfilled and a reason to get up in the morning.

A New Chapter: From Nurse to Nature Lover

Meet Elaine, a dedicated nurse for over 35 years, whose identity was deeply tied to her profession. Retirement came as a relief from the demanding schedules, but soon brought on restlessness. With no early morning rounds or patient care, she found herself searching for meaning beyond her nursing career. On a whim, Elaine joined a nature photography class, a new venture that was both challenging and exciting. Her initial attempts were far from perfect, but perseverance paid off as she found peace and joy in capturing the quiet beauty of nature. Photography became more than a hobby; it transformed her perspective and provided a new sense of identity and fulfillment.

From Career to Curiosity: Discovering New Paths

Like Elaine, retirement opens doors to explore interests that might have been sidelined due to career demands. With no alarm clocks or deadlines, this chapter of life invites you to dive into passions that elicit joy and curiosity. It's a time to shift focus from external achievements to personal satisfaction, rediscovering hobbies that once seemed unreachable. This period is about the freedom to experiment and the thrill of new experiences, which sharpen the mind and improve well-being.

Have you ever wondered what sparks joy for you now, in this chapter of your life? What's something you've always wanted to try but never had the time for?

Expert Insight: The Benefits of Exploring New Passions

One of my favorite TV experts is Dr. Sanjay Gupta. He's not just knowledgeable but has a real gift for breaking down complex ideas into terms we can all understand—and what I admire most is that you can tell he genuinely cares about people. I remember him saying, "The brain thrives on novelty and challenge," which really stuck with me. The science behind this is both fascinating and encouraging. Our brains aren't these fixed, unchanging organs; they're capable of remarkable adaptability through something called neuroplasticity. Neuroplasticity allows the brain to reorganize itself by forming new neural connections throughout our lives. This means that even in retirement, we can keep growing, rewiring our minds with new learning and experiences.

Engaging in novel activities—whether learning a musical instrument, taking up photography, or trying a new language—stimulates brain functions across multiple areas. As we challenge our minds, the brain strengthens pathways and creates new ones, improving cognitive agility. These enriched neural networks are essential in supporting memory, problem-solving, and overall mental health.

How Neuroplasticity Works and Why It Matters

Now, don't let the big word scare you—neuroplasticity sounds like something out of a science lab, but it's just the brain's way of keeping things fresh. Imagine it as the ultimate mental workout plan, where the brain flexes and rewires with each new thing you learn or experience. Even better? It's built-in, available at any age!

Neuroplasticity—your brain's ability to adapt and rewire itself—is the science behind lifelong learning. When you try something new, like learning guitar or a new language, your brain creates new pathways that strengthen with repetition. This keeps your mind sharp and resilient, no matter your age.

As Dr. Andrew Huberman explains,
"Neuroplasticity is the nervous system's ability to change in response to experience—and it's the basis for learning new things at any age."

That's why exploring new passions in retirement isn't just fun—it's a proven way to protect cognitive health and rediscover your sense of purpose.

It's an empowering reminder that reinvention isn't reserved for the young. Your brain is still wired to grow, adapt, and evolve—meaning it's never too late to explore, learn, and thrive.

The Power of Exploring New Hobbies

And these changes don't just stay in the lab—they show up in everyday hobbies. When retirees engage in new hobbies, they are making a strategic choice to support brain health while enhancing their quality of life. Pursuing an interest isn't just a way to pass time; it's an investment in well-being. Activities that require active problem-solving or involve sensory learning, like cooking, gardening, or painting are particularly beneficial, as they engage multiple parts of the brain simultaneously.

And here's one of the biggest advantages of discovering new interests today— technology makes

it easier than ever. With resources like online communities, apps, and virtual classes, you have countless opportunities to explore without even leaving home. You could join a virtual cooking class, learn an instrument through an app, or pick up photography tips from online groups. This digital age gives us freedom to try just about anything, so even if something feels like a stretch, there's likely a platform out there to help you get started.

Let's talk about learning a new language. Now, I know it might seem like a major undertaking, especially after a certain age—trust me, I get it! But here's the fun part: learning a language gives your brain an all-in-one workout, flexing memory, attention, and reasoning. As you go, your brain starts making shortcuts, making everything click faster.

Now, I won't sugarcoat it—studies do show that picking up a new language can be trickier as we get older. Sorry, it's true! But here's the twist: older adults often end up being great language learners, especially in reading, writing, and comprehension. Why? We tend to have a bit more patience, a touch more discipline, and sometimes even a more strategic approach than younger folks.

So, yes, learning a language might be harder as we age, but the brain is still totally up for the challenge. With a little grit and the right strategies, we can make it happen— and maybe even surprise ourselves along the way!

Similarly, artistic pursuits like painting or photography encourage visual processing and creative thinking, stimulating both hemispheres of the brain. In short, exploring new hobbies is a proactive way to keep the brain engaged, maintain sharpness, and foster a more fulfilling retirement journey.

Embracing Change and Staying Sharp

Embracing new challenges in retirement is not only a source of joy and personal growth but a critical element of cognitive health. By creating new connections and reinforcing old ones, retirees can cultivate an agile mind capable of adapting to new experiences and reducing stress.

Rediscovering Old Passions: A Source of Joy

Sometimes fulfillment in retirement comes from reigniting past passions. Take Harold, for example. Before his long career in corporate operations, Harold had started out as a high school teacher. Though he shifted to the business world for financial reasons, he never forgot the joy of being in a classroom. Years into retirement, he began volunteering at a local community center, helping adult learners prepare for their GEDs. That familiar spark returned. Teaching once again gave him a sense of purpose, connection, and impact. It reminded him that some passions never truly fade—they just wait patiently to be picked back up.

Rediscovering Old Passions: The Key to Lasting Fulfillment

Sometimes, the most powerful discoveries come from looking back. Research from the *Journal of Positive Psychology* reveals that retirees who actively pursue old hobbies report a 25% increase in life satisfaction. These activities, once familiar, can bring a sense of joy and purpose that feels like reconnecting with an old friend. Embracing a past passion doesn't just fill time—it reinvigorates the spirit, reminding you of the unique energy these activities once brought into your life.

Let's introduce Joan, a store manager for nearly 40 years. Retirement initially felt like a void for her until she rediscovered her love for dancing. Joan joined a local ballroom dancing class and found herself completely immersed in the rhythm and movement. Dancing reignited a creative part of her that she had long neglected, bringing a new sense of joy and fulfillment into her post-career life.

Rediscovering an old passion is like giving your past self a nod of appreciation. It's a way to honor the interests that once brought you joy—reminders of what made you feel alive before career or family took center stage.

Revisiting these activities can reveal unexpected directions for this new phase of life. As psychologist Dr. Susan Whitbourne notes, "Returning to activities from our youth can restore vitality and provide the sense of mastery that we miss when stepping away from careers."

So, as you explore what's next, don't hesitate to dust off that guitar, pick up that paintbrush, or revisit a passion that may be waiting for you. Sometimes what you've been searching for has just been waiting quietly in the wings.

The Role of Technology: Expanding Horizons

In today's digital age, technology is a powerful ally in your journey of exploration. Platforms like Meetup connect you with communities, while apps like Duolingo and Skillshare make learning new skills accessible. Technology bridges the gap between curiosity and opportunity, offering endless avenues to explore passions and expand your horizons.

The Role of Lifelong Learning: Embracing Growth in Retirement

One of the most exciting parts of retirement is the opportunity to reignite your curiosity and become a lifelong learner. With no career deadlines looming or professional responsibilities dictating your schedule, this chapter of life presents a unique opportunity to explore new subjects, acquire new skills, and challenge yourself in ways that you may have never considered before.

The research is clear: learning doesn't stop after you leave the workforce. In fact, studies show that continuous learning improves cognitive health, increases emotional resilience, and even contributes to greater longevity and overall life satisfaction.

This exercise aims to help you rediscover curiosity as a guiding force, allowing you to reconnect with interests you may have set aside. By diving into this exercise, you take active steps toward finding purpose and fulfillment, moving beyond simply "filling the days" and toward building a meaningful new identity.

Exploring Your Inner
Landscape of Curiosity

Q Reflect on
   Curiosities

🚩 Set a
   Challenge

☑ Track Your
   Progress

💬 Share Your
   Journey

Exploring Your Inner Landscape of Curiosity

The goal of this exercise is to help you open the door to new experiences, perspectives, and passions. Engaging with your curiosity is a tool to enhance mental sharpness, discover hidden talents, and increase emotional satisfaction. Without purpose, retirees are at a higher risk of depression, loneliness, and even cognitive decline, as studies on well-being show. So, let's begin the journey toward a fulfilling, curiosity-driven retirement.

Step 1: Reflect on Curiosities

✦ **Purpose:** The first step is about self-reflection. Think back to interests you've had in the past, those "what if" hobbies or dreams you never explored because of the demands of career and family.

✦ **Exercise:** Write down at least three things you've always been curious about. They don't need to be career-focused or "productive." For example, maybe you've always wanted to learn Italian, explore gardening, or try your hand at painting. Go with whatever truly excites or intrigues you.

✦ **Example:** If you're drawn to culinary arts, think back to why. Maybe you watched cooking shows but never had time to experiment. Now you can explore that interest in depth, experimenting with new recipes, learning about global cuisines, or even taking an online class.

✦ **Risk of Skipping:** Ignoring this step may leave you feeling adrift, unsure of what fulfills you in this new stage. Without a sense of direction, curiosity often fades, leaving a gap where purpose and passion could flourish.

Step 2: Set a Challenge

✦ **Purpose:** This step is about commitment. You'll choose one of your interests to focus on, making it a priority rather than a passing thought. Consistent engagement with an interest allows it to develop into a passion, bringing structure and satisfaction to your routine.

- ✦ **Exercise:** Pick one curiosity from your list and make a three-month commitment. Break it down into manageable, weekly goals that will keep you engaged and motivated. If cooking is your chosen interest, set a weekly goal of trying a new recipe, experimenting with an unfamiliar ingredient, or learning a technique, like homemade pasta-making.

- ✦ **Example:** Let's say you're interested in photography. Start with weekly goals, such as learning basic camera functions, practicing shots around your neighborhood, and building a small portfolio. You might even join a local photography group or take a workshop for hands-on experience.

- ✦ **Risk of Skipping:** Without a structured commitment, it's easy to lose momentum. The interest may feel fleeting, and you'll miss the opportunity to deepen your engagement and build a rewarding skill or hobby.

Step 3: Track Your Progress

- ✦ **Purpose:** This step encourages reflection and self-awareness. By documenting your journey, you'll have a record of how you're evolving and the impact this new pursuit has on your well-being.

- ✦ **Exercise:** Keep a journal or a digital log to track not only what you did but how each activity made you feel. Note moments of joy, challenges, and any lessons learned. Over time, this will show you patterns, helping you understand what resonates with you and what doesn't.

- ✦ **Example:** If you're exploring painting, note the satisfaction of learning new techniques, the frustration with initial mistakes, and the joy of creating something beautiful. You may notice that the process itself, more than the end product, is where you find fulfillment.

- ✦ **Risk of Skipping:** Skipping this reflection process may prevent you from fully realizing the value of the experience. Without tracking, you may overlook moments of growth, struggle to see patterns, and fail to acknowledge the progress that fuels motivation.

Step 4: Share Your Journey

- ✦ **Purpose:** Sharing connects you with others and creates a sense of accountability and community. Engaging with people who have similar interests can expand your horizons, introduce you to new ideas, and deepen your connection to the activity.

- ✦ **Exercise:** Seek out a group or individual with whom you can share your journey. This could be a local class, an online community, or even a close friend with similar interests. Share your experiences, celebrate achievements, and learn from others' perspectives.

- ✦ **Example:** If gardening is your new passion, join a local gardening club or an online community where members exchange advice, troubleshoot issues, and celebrate each season's harvest. Sharing your progress may lead to unexpected friendships, resources, or opportunities to deepen your knowledge.

- ✦ **Risk of Skipping:** When you go it alone, you may feel isolated or lose interest over time. Without the encouragement and insights of others, it's harder to sustain enthusiasm, and you miss out on the sense of connection and shared growth that enriches the journey.

Finding Purpose: The Long-Term Rewards of Curiosity

Engaging with curiosity and exploring new passions is more than a way to fill time; it's a gateway to a more purposeful life. Purpose doesn't need to look like a grand mission; it can be as simple as pursuing activities that make you feel alive, excited, and connected. Research shows that retirees who maintain a sense of purpose experience better mental health, lower rates of cognitive decline, and increased life satisfaction. Dr. Carol Ryff, a psychologist known for her work on well-being, states, "Purpose is a psychological anchor—without it, many of us feel lost, drifting without a clear direction."

As you explore your interests and passions, you build a life filled with meaning and depth. It's this commitment to personal growth that ultimately turns curiosity into a new identity and opens doors you may never have anticipated. The risks of not finding purpose are real—boredom, loneliness, and a sense of stagnation can weigh heavily on anyone unprepared for the psychological shifts of retirement. But by following your curiosity, you're actively shaping a fulfilling new chapter, one filled with personal joy, connections, and a renewed sense of who you are.

So, take this journey seriously, knowing that the purpose you create now will serve as a compass through the years ahead. Retirement, after all, is not about slowing down but about finding new ways to ignite your passions and connect with what truly matters.

A Lighter Take: *Ferris Bueller's Day Off* and the Joy of Spontaneity

Remember *Ferris Bueller's Day Off*? Ferris convinces his reluctant friend Cameron to ditch school and go on a spontaneous adventure—and by the end, Cameron's the one who grows the most. That's retirement in a nutshell: stepping away from rigid routines and saying yes to curiosity and the unknown. Like Cameron, you might resist at first, but some of the most rewarding experiences come when you loosen the grip on structure and follow where joy and spontaneity lead.

The Real Power of Staying Connected: Relationships Fuel Passion

As we move into this next phase of life, staying connected to people is just as important as exploring new passions. You don't have to go it alone. Whether it's joining a class, reconnecting with old friends, or mentoring someone, relationships fuel our passion and give deeper meaning to what we do.

Conclusion: The Adventure Continues

Reflecting on my own journey, some of my most meaningful connections came from following a curiosity and sharing it with others. By opening myself up to new experiences, I met people with similar interests, and soon I had a new circle that brought a renewed sense of purpose. So, as you dive into this adventure, remember—you don't have to do it alone.

Retirement is your opportunity to redefine success through joy, curiosity, and connection. Embrace the freedom to explore, letting each discovery enrich this new chapter. Whether it's learning an instrument, picking up a new sport, or finally tackling a long-desired pursuit, retirement holds endless possibilities waiting to be embraced.

Chapter 6 Takeaways: Exploring New Passions – Turning Curiosity into Purpose

RTF Step 4: Exploring New Passions and Purpose

- ☑ Purpose in retirement often begins with curiosity—it grows through action, reflection, and exploration.

- ☑ Both rediscovering old passions and trying new ones can reignite joy, identity, and meaning.

- ☑ New hobbies are more than entertainment—they support cognitive health, emotional resilience, and mental sharpness.

- ☑ Lifelong learning keeps the brain adaptable and engaged—your mind is wired to grow at any age.

- ☑ Technology makes it easier than ever to explore new interests and connect with others who share them.

- ☑ Sharing your journey with others builds community, adds accountability, and multiplies the joy of discovery.

❋ **What's Next in the RTF Journey?**

In Chapter 7, we'll explore **Strengthening Relationships – Building a Connected Retirement**, and why human connection is essential for a purpose-driven life.

Each step forward lays a stronger foundation for a fulfilling retirement. Now that we've explored the importance of passion and purpose, it's time to focus on the relationships that truly matter. In Chapter 7, *Strengthening Relationships – Building a Connected Retirement*, we'll dive into how nurturing bonds with family, friends, and new acquaintances can bring deeper meaning and joy to this next phase. Let's continue by discovering how to build a supportive community around you.

Strengthening Relationships – Building a Connected Retirement

What you will learn: The quality of your retirement is shaped by the quality of your relationships—invest in them.

""The key to healthy aging is relationships, relationships, relationships."
— *Dr. George Vaillant*

What If Relationships Were the Real Key to a Happy Retirement?

Picture this: you've finally reached retirement, kicked off those work shoes, and now you have all the free time you could ever want. But with all that freedom, you might find yourself wondering how to fill those hours meaningfully. The answer often lies in something simple yet profound, relationships. In retirement, more than ever, it's about surrounding yourself with people who bring joy, laughter, and a sense of belonging.

What relationships come to mind for you? Who are the people you're eager to reconnect with or spend more time around?

Research shows that social connections play a significant role in overall happiness, especially as we age. A recent AARP survey revealed that nearly 60% of retirees reported feeling happier after reconnecting with friends and family they had lost touch with over the years. And while it might feel daunting to rekindle those old bonds or build new ones, the effort is well worth it. Relationships offer a sense of continuity, anchoring us as we step into new routines and sometimes into the unknown. Building and nurturing them adds layers to our lives, giving each day more purpose.

In this chapter, we'll explore how to rekindle old relationships, navigate the new dynamics of retirement, and even bridge the technological gap between you and the younger generation (yeah it happens). Plus, we'll dive into the benefits of play, shared activities, and personal stories, showing you that it's never too late to rebuild or strengthen meaningful connections. Whether you're starting from scratch or revitalizing long-standing bonds, this chapter will guide you through the joy and fulfillment that come from a connected life.

Starting Fresh: Morning Rituals That Reconnect

Let's be honest, when you first retire, your daily routine gets flipped upside down. Without a commute or a packed schedule, you may find yourself sipping coffee at the kitchen table, wondering what's next. One retiree described his first morning off as accidentally dressing up in his old work clothes because his body was so used to the routine! For some, that disorientation fades quickly, but for others, the change can feel like a hole in the day.

How would you want to start your day? What would make the morning feel worthwhile?

For George and Linda, the sudden shift meant more time together but also an opportunity to form new rituals. After years of starting their mornings separately, George began to feel restless in retirement. Then, one morning, Linda decided to join him for coffee on the porch. This simple ritual became a daily habit where they would sit together, enjoy the quiet, and reconnect. Little by little, it brought them closer, helping them rediscover the simple joy of each other's company. Sometimes, just starting the day together became the touchstone that set a positive tone for both.

Let me share a simple connection I made right in our own neighborhood. We live in a newly built community, so meeting new neighbors is a regular thing. One morning while I was out walking our dogs, I spotted a guy—Kevin—detailing a car in his driveway, with a small sign advertising his services.

Naturally, I stopped to chat. Kevin told me he had recently retired from the car business and started detailing cars just to stay active and meet people in the neighborhood. What began as a side hobby quickly turned into a real passion. For him, it wasn't just about cleaning cars—it gave him structure, a sense of pride, and the satisfaction of seeing his work appreciated. Oh, and the extra cash didn't hurt either.

Talking to Kevin reminded me how meaningful it can be to build relationships and find shared interests close to home. I didn't have the heart to tell him the HOA technically doesn't allow home businesses in the driveway—but hey, he's happy, the cars look great, and the neighbors love him. Just like George and Linda's new morning ritual, Kevin's car detailing has become his way of staying connected and enjoying retirement with a fresh sense of purpose.

Expert Insight: The Power of Shared Rituals

Relationship expert Dr. John Gottman emphasizes the importance of rituals in maintaining strong connections. According to him, shared rituals like George and

Linda's coffee mornings build a sense of predictability and bonding. "Even small rituals strengthen relationships by creating shared moments of connection," he explains. Whether it's a weekly movie night, a daily walk, or even cooking a meal together, these rituals are crucial in retirement when the old routines fade away, but the need for connection remains. As simple as they seem, these small acts can offer stability and deeper bonding.

Recap: Why New Routines Matter

Building new routines in retirement is more than just filling time—it's about creating intentional moments with the people we care about. Simple rituals can become cherished parts of the day, offering stability and a sense of shared experience that can make all the difference in your connection. When we craft these routines, we're also inviting others into our new phase, giving everyone involved a shared ground to look forward to each day.

The Technology Tangle: Bridging the Generational Gap

Navigating technology can feel like a minefield, but it's a powerful tool for staying connected with family. If you're struggling with FaceTime or accidentally live streaming your cat on Facebook, you're not alone. Joan, a retired teacher, became a self-declared "Tech Granny" after a string of hilarious tech mishaps. Determined to keep up with her grandkids, she embraced FaceTime, texting, and even emoji-filled messages. What began as a blunder turned into a family joke—and a new way to bond. Her grandkids came to love her enthusiastic, if not always successful, video chats.

Do you have family members who seem light-years ahead of you with tech? How might learning their ways add a new dynamic to your relationship?

Expert Insight: Learning Tech for Connection and Cognitive Health

Dr. Gary Small, a neuroscientist, shares that mastering new technologies in retirement does more than just help you stay in touch—it strengthens cognitive health. "Learning technology not only gives older adults a sense of accomplishment but also provides fresh ways to connect with loved ones," he notes. So, whether you're figuring out TikTok or setting up a Zoom call, you're engaging with family and exercising your brain. And that's the beauty of it—learning tech doesn't just bridge the distance; it challenges your mind, keeping it sharp and active in an era when you want to stay connected.

Recap: Technology as a Connection Tool

While it may feel awkward at first, learning to navigate tech can be one of the best decisions for staying connected. It's a skill that opens doors to frequent communication with family and friends, bridging gaps across generations and helping you stay engaged with the people who matter most. By conquering these digital "mountains," you're also giving yourself more agency and flexibility in the way you interact with others, even if they're on the other side of the world.

The Technology Tangle

Navigating technology can feel like a minefield, but it's a powerful tool for staying connected with family.

Tech Mishaps	Tech Wins
Struggling with FaceTime	Enjoying a video chat
Accidentally live streaming on Facebook	Posting photos to social media
Texting your grandkids with typos	Texting your grandkids with emojis
Texting your grandkids with emojis	Burking photos formulvened

Rediscovering Fun Together: The Power of Play

Retirement is a time to bring fun back into your relationships, whether through hobbies, games, or spontaneous adventures. Bob and Mary, for instance, joined a painting class together, sparking a light-hearted debate about art that deepened their bond.

Personally, one of my most memorable bonding experiences was a bit of an initiation into the corporate world, though not in the way you might expect. Right after college, I landed a spot in a training program, supposedly preparing me to run a branch office someday. Little did I know, operations was not my calling. I'm about as detail oriented as a cat chasing a laser pointer! Thankfully, Kip Whitefield, the VP of sales, saw potential in me. He took me on a local sales call and, by some miracle, pegged me as a salesperson. He must've seen the wild-eyed ambition or just plain desperation to escape operations because a few months later, he hand-picked me for his national sales team, relocating me from Chicago to sunny Orange County, California.

Suddenly, I was thrust from handling order forms and dispatch schedules to selling at corporate HQs. I'd gone from a steady (if slightly mundane) gig to being the kid on the big stage in an LA-based corporate sales role. The thrill was real... and so was the terror. "Fly or die" became my mantra, though every time I repeated it, I felt I might do the latter.

Humor in Building Connections: My First Day at Transamerica Occidental

When Kip finally left me on my own after a few client intros, my first solo pitch was to Transamerica Occidental Life Insurance. I was 25, barely trained for this, and more than a little freaked out. I'd been up half the night, mentally running through all the questions they might ask—the kind that would make me sweat or, worse, leave me with no answer at all. After a two-hour crawl on the LA freeway, I parked and walked toward the towering skyscraper. I craned my neck, looking up at the huge building that stretched into the sky, questioning every decision I'd made to get here. 'I'm going to be sick,' I thought. But after a few deep breaths and a half-hearted attempt to calm myself with my "fly or die" mantra, I went in.

Midway through my second meeting, I was sweating bullets as I sat across from Chuck Lilly, the no-nonsense head of vendor quality and costs, when his phone rang. He put down the phone, looked at me, and said, "Lloyd Von Sprecken wants to meet with you now." Now? I wasn't scheduled to meet Lloyd until later that afternoon. I'd heard everything about him from Kip: "head of Life Underwriting, a tough customer, and a character" (sales-speak for he's going to mess with you). Just what I needed on Day One. They led me through a maze of buildings, pointing out something unique as we went: both buildings were set on wheels, resting in a massive two-foot rubber buffer so they could rock and roll during earthquakes. In the event of a quake, these entire buildings would sway gently back and forth to absorb the shock. Earthquakes?! I thought. Now I have to worry about the buildings shaking and rolling too?

Lloyd turned out to be unexpectedly friendly, though. "Let's go to lunch," he said. "Your COO Glen Smith is one of my favorites." That's a promising start, right? We headed across the street to a dive bar, classic LA style. The place looked like it was held together by duct tape and dirt, and just as we walked in, this elderly waitress named Bulla—who looked like she'd been there since Hollywood was still farmland—greeted us. Lloyd introduced me, saying, "This is Dave. He's new here."

Bulla, sizing me up, deadpanned, "Seen the art on the back of our front door yet?" I turned around and before I could respond, I felt two claws firmly pinch both my butt cheeks. "Welcome to the club!" she grinned, while Lloyd laughed so hard I thought he might fall off his stool. Apparently, this was Lloyd's unofficial initiation—pure corporate hazing wrapped in an innocent lunch invitation.

After that "warm" welcome, lunch turned out to be great. Lloyd was supportive, Bulla went easy on me the rest of the time, and I left the dive bar with a better perspective. That day taught me a lesson that stuck with me: no matter how terrifying a business situation seems, most of them turn out just fine if you can muster the courage to walk in. After all, if you can survive a surprise squeeze from Bulla and keep your cool, you can survive anything. Fly or die, right?

Recap: Why Play Matters in Relationships

Bringing playfulness back into relationships provides more than just entertainment—it strengthens bonds, builds empathy, and creates shared experiences that keep relationships vibrant. Laughter, play, and fun serve as natural ways to keep connections engaging and lighthearted. By making time for these playful interactions, you're fostering a relationship that's resilient and rich in shared joy.

Bob and Mary, for instance, joined a painting class together. Bob, ever the meticulous engineer, approached each brushstroke with precision, while Mary embraced abstract splashes of color. Their painting sessions turned into light-hearted debates about art techniques, punctuated by laughter, deepening their bond. Trying something new together, like this, adds an element of playfulness, reminding them that their relationship is about more than just history—it's about shared growth and fun too.

What would bring a smile to your face? Is there something you've always wanted to try together?

Expert Commentary: The Benefits of Play in Relationships

Dr. Stuart Brown, founder of the National Institute for Play, emphasizes the role of play in maintaining healthy relationships. "Play reduces stress, encourages empathy, and fosters connection," he explains. Activities like painting, dancing, or even trying new recipes can inject fun into your relationships and keep things fresh, especially when routines are changing. Dr. Brown adds that couples who play together experience fewer conflicts and are better at resolving issues when they do arise. Play introduces levity and joy, making it a powerful way to fortify bonds that might otherwise grow routine.

Personal Story: Reconnecting with My Brother, Tom

My brother Tom, who's nine years older than me, was someone I always looked up to as a kid. Even though he was often off doing his own thing, I cherished the times he came home and shared stories. He was part of the 'hippie' era—long hair, rock bands, the whole scene. I remember one visit to see him in Chicago when he was living with his bandmates in an enormous old house. They didn't have much, just a mattress on the floor and the bare essentials. I was young and seeing him so skinny and living like that scared me. I didn't understand why he was living that way, but he was still my big brother, and I admired him.

Fast forward about 20 years, and we both found ourselves married. Somehow, misunderstandings and hurt feelings created a rift between us, and we drifted apart. The reasons don't seem to matter much anymore. And to be honest, I don't remember every detail—just enough to know that our perspectives on what happened are probably very different. Vicky, Tom's wife, was involved—just as my ex-wife was too. Looking back, it was never just one person's story. We each had a part in how things played out. After all those years, I knew reconnecting with Tom, Vicky, and their family was a priority for me, so I made it one of my retirement goals.

When we finally reconnected a few years ago, it was clear Vicky still had things she wanted to say. It wasn't easy for any of us, but we decided not to dwell on the past and instead to look forward. Suzanne and I even flew to Oregon to surprise Tom for his birthday. I walked into the restaurant wearing a ridiculous mask—a nod to a character from Men in Black—with a pair of testicles hanging from the chin. The reactions from other patrons were priceless, and when I took the mask off, Tom's surprise turned into laughter.

We've kept things light since then, focusing on staying in touch and sharing in each other's lives again. We text, call, and visit when we can, even though we're on opposite coasts. Reconnecting with Tom and his family has been one of the fulfilling parts of this new chapter of my life.

Recap: Reconnecting with Family

Sometimes, rekindling relationships means putting aside old misunderstandings and embracing a shared future. By reconnecting with my brother, I rediscovered the importance of family bonds, no matter how different our lives became. Each message or call is a reminder that family ties are powerful and worth nurturing, even if they've faced ups and downs.

Practical Exercises: Strengthening Relationships in Retirement

Strengthening relationships in retirement isn't just about passing the time; it's about building a strong, reliable support network that provides emotional fulfillment, reduces feelings of isolation, and enhances mental and physical well-being. Retirement offers a unique chance to reestablish, deepen, and enrich relationships, creating bonds that will add value, purpose, and joy to this stage of life. Here are three intentional exercises designed to help you reconnect, deepen, and maintain meaningful connections.

Practical Exercises:
Strengthening Relationships in Retirement

Create New Rituals Together
Start regular activities like weekly game nights or daily walks with your partner.

Embrace Technology with Family
Learn a new tech skill, such as making video calls with your grandchildren.

Rekindle Old Friendships and Family Ties
Reach out to someone you haven't seen in a while and rebuild the connection

1. Create New Rituals Together

✦ **Exercise:** Establish regular, consistent activities, such as a weekly family game night, Sunday brunch with friends, or daily walks with your partner. The key here is to select activities that everyone enjoys and looks forward to. If mobility or location is a factor, consider adapting the activity—like a virtual coffee catch-up or a shared weekly movie watched from separate locations but discussed together afterward. This can be as simple or as elaborate as you like, as long as it becomes a routine.

✦ **Impact:** Establishing these regular, consistent connections can lower stress, create a sense of normalcy, and significantly reduce feelings of loneliness—benefits that are often crucial in retirement. These rituals, whether big or small, act as emotional anchors, providing a source of joy, stability, and support. They also foster a sense of predictability and connection, making your relationships an anticipated, reassuring part of each week. Studies indicate that regular social engagement can help prevent depression and bolster resilience, reinforcing that even a small weekly gathering can have substantial, lasting benefits.

2. **Embrace Technology with Family**

   ✦ **Exercise:** Step out of your comfort zone and learn a new tech skill alongside a family member or friend. Try video calls with grandchildren, create a family photo album to share with loved ones, or dive into social media to stay up-to-date and interact with family near and far. If the learning curve feels challenging, invite a family member to coach you or take a course together. Mastering the nuances of technology becomes an adventure and can also be a bonding experience, where you learn and laugh together.

   ✦ **Goal:** Successfully use your new tech skill to stay connected with family members at least once a week. This could mean a video call on Sundays, posting photos, sharing updates, or even leaving voice messages for a loved one. Not only does this keep you involved in their lives, but it also bridges the generational gap, strengthening bonds across ages. Mastering technology has a dual benefit: it helps to build and maintain relationships while keeping your brain sharp. Research has shown that learning new skills, particularly in technology, can enhance cognitive agility and improve memory, adding layers of value to each interaction.

3. **Rekindle Old Friendships and Family Ties**

   ✦ **Exercise:** Reaching out to someone you haven't spoken with in a long time, whether a high school friend, a former coworker, or an old family friend, can feel daunting. Begin by sending a warm, simple message, expressing genuine interest in reconnecting. Once you re-establish contact, make an effort to schedule regular calls, meet-ups, or even written correspondence. Try to set a monthly lunch date or a weekly call to build consistency into this rekindled connection, which will allow the relationship to grow naturally over time.

   ✦ **Goal:** Aim to rebuild at least one meaningful connection with a friend or family member over the next three months. These revived relationships often carry shared histories, creating a unique blend of familiarity and nostalgia that enriches your life. Over time, this consistent interaction provides emotional support, laughter, and a comforting sense of continuity. Reaching out can offer a renewed sense of purpose and introduce fresh perspectives, making you feel valued and giving you the chance to provide the same in return. According to studies, maintaining friendships can improve life satisfaction, reduce stress, and offer practical health benefits, reminding us that the relationships we revive today can become cherished parts of our lives going forward.

Conclusion: The Power of Connection in Retirement

In the end, the real treasure of retirement isn't just the freedom to do what you want—it's the people you get to share it with. It's the friends who still get your jokes, the family who shows up, the neighbor who waves every morning. These relationships—old and new, simple and deep—are what make this chapter richer and more meaningful. So, invest in them. Rekindle old bonds. Spark new ones. Laugh together. Learn together. That's how we build a connected, fulfilling life after work—one relationship at a time.

On my own journey, some of the most fulfilling moments didn't come from doing things alone—but from saying yes to shared experiences. A curiosity here, a conversation there—and suddenly, new friendships, new energy, and a renewed sense of purpose emerged.

Retirement is your chance to redefine success—not through titles or trophies, but through joy, connection, and growth. Whether you're picking up a new hobby, mentoring someone younger, or just spending more time with people who lift you up, each step forward strengthens the foundation of a life well lived.

Chapter 7 Takeaways: Strengthening Relationships – Building a Connected Retirement

RTF Step 5: Deepening Social Connections for a Purpose-Filled Life

✅ Retirement isn't just about free time—it's about who you spend that time with. Invest in relationships that bring you joy, purpose, and connection.

✅ Simple daily rituals like morning coffee or a weekly call can anchor your day and strengthen bonds with loved ones.

✅ Learning technology may feel intimidating, but it's one of the best tools for staying connected—while giving your brain a workout at the same time.

✅ Play and laughter aren't just for kids. Shared fun—whether through hobbies, games, or inside jokes—keeps relationships fresh and meaningful.

✅ Reconnecting with family and old friends can bring closure, healing, and a renewed sense of belonging—don't wait for "someday."

✅ Strong relationships in retirement improve mental health, boost resilience, and reduce loneliness—your circle is your superpower.

✺ What's Next in the RTF Journey?

Up next: **Chapter 8 – Leaving a Legacy: Making a Lasting Impact.**

We'll explore how to turn your experiences, wisdom, and generosity into a lasting contribution through family, mentorship, or community involvement. Because fulfillment doesn't end with connection—it grows stronger when you share it forward.

Leaving a Legacy –
Making a Lasting Impact

What you will learn: Legacy isn't about wealth—it's about how you live, lead, and love today.

"Carve your name on hearts, not tombstones. A legacy is etched into the minds of others and the stories they share about you."
— Shannon L. Alder

What Will You Be Remembered For?

Imagine this: you're at your 100th birthday celebration, surrounded by family, friends, and maybe even a few surprise guests. I hope to make it to that age! They're sharing stories, recounting your quirks, your achievements, and the unique ways you impacted their lives. What do you hope they'll say? Will it be about the laughter you shared, the guidance you offered, or the way you showed up when they needed you most?

Leaving a legacy isn't just about what you accumulate; it's about the mark you leave on others and the world. With retirement comes the unique opportunity to reflect on how you want to be remembered, and more importantly, to start creating that legacy now. In this chapter, we'll explore how you can make a meaningful, lasting impact—one that resonates long after you're gone.

The Ghost of Legacy Yet to Come: *A Christmas Carol*

In *A Christmas Carol*, Scrooge is given a haunting glimpse into his future—a legacy marked by loneliness and indifference. He realizes too late that his life, as it was, made no real impact on the people around him.

Thankfully, your retirement probably won't come with ghostly visitors (fingers crossed!). But the message still hits home: how we live today shapes how we're remembered tomorrow.

Legacy isn't some distant, lofty goal—it's built step-by-step, through everyday moments of kindness, connection, and contribution. No spirits required.

The Power of Legacy: Facts and Figures

If you're wondering just how important legacy is, consider this: research by Merrill Lynch found that nearly 65% of retirees say they want to make a difference in the world. Another study published in *Psychological Science* reveals that older adults with a sense of legacy have higher life satisfaction and emotional well-being. Yet, only about 30% feel they've achieved this goal, according to a *Journal of Aging Studies* article.

The desire to leave a legacy is shared by many, but the gap between wanting to make an impact and doing so can feel wide. This chapter is about bridging that gap and helping you to actively shape your legacy, whether it's through family, community, or even the causes you support.

Celebrity Perspectives: Famous Legacies

Many well-known figures have contemplated their legacies in retirement, each leaving a unique mark:

✦ **Oprah Winfrey**: After decades on television, Oprah shifted her focus toward education and empowerment. Her legacy lives on through the Oprah Winfrey Leadership Academy for Girls in South Africa, which provides education and support to underserved young women.

✦ **Jimmy Carter**: Following his presidency, Carter dedicated his time to humanitarian work through the Carter Center, focusing on human rights and public health. His legacy is one of service, showing that even after a high-profile career, new paths for impact remain.

✦ **Bill Gates**: Although he's best known for founding Microsoft, Gates has devoted his post-retirement years to philanthropy through the Bill & Melinda Gates Foundation. His legacy isn't just in technology but in his commitment to global health and education.

These folks show us that a real legacy isn't about awards or recognition. It's about rolling up your sleeves, taking action, and making a difference in a way that feels right to you.

Everyday Examples: Leaving a Legacy Without Fame or Fortune

Listen though, legacy isn't exclusive to the wealthy or famous; it's something anyone can build through everyday actions. It's about courage, kindness, family values, and the positive impact you have on those around you.

"What you leave behind is not what is engraved in stone monuments, but what is woven into the lives of others." – Pericles

Here are some inspiring examples of ordinary people who have made extraordinary contributions:

Oseola McCarty – The Humble Philanthropist

A washerwoman from Mississippi, Oseola McCarty saved and donated $150,000 to the University of Southern Mississippi to fund scholarships for African American students. Despite her modest income, her commitment to education and generosity left a profound legacy, inspiring others to contribute to educational causes.

Fun Fact:
She never owned a car or a television, yet she quietly saved enough money to endow a college scholarship fund that changed lives.

Planting Trees in Old Age – Anonymous Forester

An elderly man from India planted thousands of trees in a barren area to combat deforestation. The forest he cultivated not only rejuvenated the local ecosystem but also provided a habitat for wildlife, creating a lasting environmental legacy.

Fun Fact:
Locals in his Indian village nicknamed the forest he created *"Molai Forest"* after him—turning his once-deserted planting area into a vibrant ecosystem visible from satellite imagery.

Eva Perón – Champion of the Underprivileged

Eva Perón, the former First Lady of Argentina, remains one of the most influential—and at times controversial—figures in Latin American history. Deeply loved by many for her efforts to uplift the poor, she became a powerful symbol of compassion and advocacy.

Through the **Eva Perón Foundation**, she spearheaded initiatives that built schools, hospitals, and housing for Argentina's most underserved citizens.

While her legacy is debated in political circles, particularly in relation to her husband's presidency, her direct contributions to improving the lives of the working class and the marginalized left a deep, lasting impact. Even today, she is remembered by many in Argentina as a voice for the voiceless—a woman who rose from humble beginnings to champion those who had long been overlooked.

Fun Fact:
She was the first woman in Argentina to appear on a banknote—an enduring symbol of her legacy among the poor and working class.

James Harrison – The Man with the Golden Arm

An Australian known as the "Man with the Golden Arm," James Harrison donated blood plasma every week for over 60 years. His donations, contained rare antibodies to help others.

Fun Fact:
His blood donations helped develop Anti-D, a treatment that has saved over 2 million babies from Rhesus disease in Australia alone.

These everyday heroes show us that building a legacy isn't about fame or fortune—it's about kindness, generosity, and staying true to what matters most to you. Legacies don't have to be big to be meaningful; they can be deeply personal, touching the lives of a whole community, your family, or even just one person. So don't let the stories of world-changing wealth or fame intimidate you. It's not about that. Like these folks, you can make an impact that feels true to who you are, no matter how small or simple it may seem.

Personal Story: My Father's Legacy

My dad served in the Navy during WWII, enlisting at just 18 years old like so many of his generation who were thrust from their daily lives into unimaginable horrors. He rarely spoke about the war, occasionally sharing a lighthearted anecdote from his days aboard the ship, but he kept the real stories - those filled with terror and hardship - locked away. I learned from my mom that his job was to ferry soldiers to the shores, directly into combat. He drove the landing crafts from ship to shore, while being relentlessly shot at and bombed. It was a role few would have chosen willingly, and I can only imagine the fear he must have felt with each trip, knowing that survival was far from guaranteed.

Years after the war, when I was just a ten-year-old kid, we visited my dad's mom, who we all called "Cookie." She still lived in the house where my dad and his siblings grew up. Being young and curious, I started poking around, and I found a stash of letters tucked away in one of her dresser drawers. These were letters my dad had written to her during the war. As I read them, I was blown away by the courage that poured out of every line. He never mentioned the danger or the fear, never hinted at the life-threatening situations he faced. Instead, he spoke of the positives - assuring her he was fine, telling her not to worry, and promising he'd be home soon.

Those letters left a lasting impression on me. They were a legacy he never knew he was leaving, a testament to the kind of man he was. In those words, I saw two powerful lessons. First, to be courageous, even when you're scared. It was clear to me that he had faced unthinkable fears, but he never let them permeate into his words to his mother. Instead, he chose to project strength, knowing that his own fears would do her no good. Second, he taught me about kindness. He was deeply aware of how worried she must have been, with two sons over there in imminent danger. And so, he tempered his own reality, offering her a version that gave her comfort and hope, at a time when both were in short supply.

To this day, those letters are a secret source of strength for me. Whenever I'm in a tough situation - not life-and-death like his but daunting all the same - I think back to the courage he showed, both in facing his own fears and in shielding his mom from them. This legacy of resilience and compassion became a gift he left only to me. My siblings, Tom and Sharon, never read those letters, but I believe he somehow left similar or other legacies to them that I know nothing about. I'm sure they carry their own hidden gifts from him, quietly guiding them through their own lives.

I wish I'd told him how much those letters meant to me before he passed, but I think he knew. In the end, legacies can be for humanity or family, and sometimes they're uniquely personal, left only for those who were meant to find them.

Just like my dad's courage and kindness left their mark on me, every one of us has a chance to think about the values we want to pass down. And really, isn't that the best gift we could leave behind? Something that keeps going, long after we're gone. So, here's my question to you: What will yours be?

Practical Steps to Build Your Legacy

Building a legacy is a journey of self-discovery, intentionality, and impact. These steps guide you through crafting a meaningful legacy that aligns with your values, extends your influence, and resonates with future generations.

1. Define What Legacy Means to You

Taking a few moments to think about what kind of legacy you want can be a real game-changer. It's not just about what you leave behind—it's how you live every day, how you show up for others, and the values you pass along.

Exercise: Reflect on and write down what you hope to be remembered for, focusing on character traits, values, and contributions that define your life's purpose. Consider the kind of influence you want to have had on others and the world.

- ✦ *Goal*: Create a concise personal mission statement for your legacy—one that captures your core values and aspirations. Keep it under three sentences for clarity, focusing on themes like integrity, compassion, or resilience.
- ✦ *Reflective Prompt*: What value or lesson would you most want others to associate with you? Imagine a message that your grandchildren or community members would remember you by—how would they describe your impact?

In-Depth Insight: Think about your own role models and what you've admired most in them. This exercise can guide you toward qualities and values you may want to emphasize in your own legacy.

2. Identify Your Sphere of Influence

Everyone has a unique sphere of influence where their actions can have an impact, from immediate family to community organizations. This step is about recognizing and intentionally engaging with those within your reach.

- ✦ *Exercise*: List specific people, groups, and causes you feel connected to or passionate about, considering how you can make a meaningful difference.

✦ *Goal*: Select at least one area or relationship in which you can begin to invest actively, whether by mentoring someone, volunteering in your community, or lending your voice to an important cause.

✦ *Reflective Prompt*: Who in your life could benefit from what you have to offer right now? Reflect on those in your network, and think about where your unique skills, knowledge, or support could have a lasting positive effect.

In-Depth Insight: Consider practical ways to start small, such as setting up monthly coffee meetings with a mentee, joining a local charity board, or volunteering with a community program. Sometimes, the simplest acts of engagement can leave the most profound impact.

3. Create Meaningful Traditions

Traditions are powerful tools for connecting across generations, reinforcing values, and creating shared memories. Even small, meaningful rituals can become cherished aspects of your legacy.

✦ *Exercise*: Reflect on possible rituals or traditions you could initiate with your family or community. This might include hosting an annual family dinner, establishing a scholarship in your name, or volunteering as a group.

✦ *Goal*: Start at least one new tradition this year that embodies your values and reinforces connection with those around you.

✦ *Reflective Prompt*: What small tradition could you start this year that would bring you closer to loved ones? Traditions don't have to be elaborate; they just need to be meaningful.

In-Depth Insight: Think of ways to include loved ones in planning these traditions to ensure they resonate with everyone involved. Family members could share in the responsibility or take turns leading the tradition, fostering deeper connections and involvement.

4. Support a Cause Close to Your Heart

Aligning your legacy with a cause that deeply resonates with you provides a tangible way to make a lasting impact beyond your immediate circle. Philanthropy or volunteering with intent can solidify your connection to your values.

- ✦ *Action*: Research organizations or causes that reflect your values. This could involve making financial contributions, volunteering, or becoming an advocate for a cause that holds special meaning to you.

- ✦ *Goal*: Establish a meaningful connection with this cause, whether through regular contributions, active participation, or by educating others about it.

- ✦ *Reflective Prompt*: What issue or cause stirs a strong emotional response in you? Reflect on moments in your life that ignited a sense of purpose or urgency. This can help reveal causes that truly resonate with your values and priorities.

In-Depth Insight: Consider leaving a legacy fund or endowment if resources allow, so your support continues even after you're gone. Alternatively, if volunteering is your focus, set a goal for regular participation and explore ways to involve family or friends, potentially inspiring them to carry on your efforts.

5. Capture Your Story

Documenting your life's journey, lessons, and experiences is a priceless gift for future generations. Sharing these stories gives insight into your values, struggles, and triumphs, offering guidance and inspiration to those who come after you.

- ✦ *Exercise*: Begin writing or recording your life story, focusing on the defining moments and lessons that shaped your values and character. This could take the form of a memoir, video, or a series of letters to loved ones.

- ✦ *Goal*: Aim to complete one chapter or recording each month. Set aside time regularly to reflect and share, building a story over time.

- ✦ *Reflective Prompt*: What single lesson or value would you want future generations to remember you for? Consider lessons learned from challenges and successes that you'd want to pass on.

In-Depth Insight: Include anecdotes, advice, and reflections on how specific values helped you navigate different stages of life. This project can be a cherished record of both your accomplishments and your growth, helping descendants understand your journey and values.

Additionally, explore creative ways to document your story, such as using photos, family recipes, or even a family tree with stories attached to each branch.

The Importance of Family Connections in Legacy-Building

Research by the Pew Research Center shows that 77% of retirees prioritize family in retirement, underscoring the vital role relationships play in building a legacy. The American Psychological Association also notes that reconnecting with family can boost emotional health, lower stress, and provide a stronger sense of belonging.

You can see that it's not just about passing on wealth or accomplishments; it's about passing on stories, values, and a sense of connection. Rebuilding family ties can be challenging, but the rewards are well worth it, offering both emotional richness and a meaningful legacy.

Conclusion: Your Legacy Begins Now

As you reflect on your journey, consider this: your legacy isn't something you leave behind—it's something you build every day. Through relationships, values, and the impact you leave on the world, your legacy is an evolving testament to who you are. Take the time to shape it intentionally, knowing that every moment you invest in others contributes to a lasting impact.

Ask yourself, what one small action could you take today to begin shaping your legacy?

Remember, leaving a meaningful impact is less about grand gestures and more about consistent, intentional actions that reflect your deepest values. Building a legacy isn't a one-time effort; it's a journey that evolves as you do. But legacy is only one part of crafting a fulfilling retirement. To fully embrace this new chapter, it's essential to adapt to the tools and opportunities available today. What do you want the story of your life to say, and how can you begin to live that story today?

🔍 Reflection Questions

1. **What do you want to be remembered for?**
   Write down the character traits, values, or contributions you hope others will associate with your name.

2. **Who in your life could benefit from your presence, wisdom, or support right now?**
   Think about where your impact could start today—with one person, one group, or one cause.

3. **Is there a tradition or story you want to pass on?**
   What moment, memory, or value from your life deserves to be shared with the next generation?

4. **What's one small action you could take this week to begin shaping your legacy?**
   Whether it's reaching out, writing a letter, or volunteering an hour—start where you are.

Chapter 8 Takeaways: Leaving a Legacy – Making a Lasting Impact

RTF Step 5: Leaving a Legacy

✅ **Legacy isn't just what you leave behind—it's how you show up every day.**
Your daily actions, words, and values shape how you'll be remembered.

✅ **You don't need money or fame to make a lasting impact.**
Ordinary people leave powerful legacies through generosity, kindness, and consistency.

✅ **Your legacy can take many forms.**
Whether it's mentoring, supporting a cause, creating family traditions, or writing down your life lessons—it's all meaningful.

✅ **Small, intentional efforts have ripple effects.**
Sharing your story, spending time with family, or planting a seed of kindness can impact generations.

✅ **The best legacies start with heart.**
Compassion, resilience, and the desire to uplift others are often the most enduring gifts you can pass on.

✸ What's Next in the RTF Journey?

In Chapter 9, *Staying Current – Adapting to Technology in Retirement*, we'll explore how to stay relevant, connected, and empowered in today's fast-moving digital world. Legacy is built through people—but it's strengthened by staying engaged with the tools of the present and future.

Staying Current – Adapting to Technology in Retirement

📍 **What you will learn:** Staying curious about technology keeps you connected, independent, and empowered in today's world.

"The future is already here; it's just unevenly distributed." –
William Ford Gibson

Let me start with some geeky "strategery!"

Probably best to begin with an example of what Gibson is talking about for clarity. Take healthcare, for instance. Advanced healthcare technology, like gene editing (CRISPR), personalized medicine, and AI-driven diagnostics, is disturbingly only accessible in top research hospitals and affluent communities. In contrast, rural or economically disadvantaged areas may still struggle with access to basic healthcare, creating an uneven distribution of medical advances.

Consider another example: while India has made strides in adding infrastructure for electricity, there are still over 10 million people in the country without access. For context, that's equivalent to the entire state of North Carolina lacking electricity in their homes. If you didn't know this fact, think about it the next time you go into a room and easily flip on a switch!

Gibson's quote really hits home for a lot of us in retirement: tech is speeding ahead, but it's not reaching everyone equally. Retirees often fall into that left-behind group. For years, most of our tech exposure came straight from the workplace. Our jobs kept us in the loop, regularly introducing new tools, software, and gadgets that quickly became part of our daily routines. And while our smartphones connect us to apps and the internet, tech is advancing fast, with things like AI set to make life both easier and, let's be honest, more confusing. But in retirement, that steady stream of updates, training, and new tech stops, making it easy to feel out of touch. Plus, we don't have the luxury of calling IT to solve our tech problems anymore. I once had a boss who, whenever his computer wouldn't work, would say, "Someone find me a guy with a ponytail!" Now, though, we're on our own, just as the world becomes even more connected and tech driven. If we're not careful, it's all too easy to feel left behind.

As a personal fan of technology myself, I'm not one to shy away from trying new tools. I have always been willing to live on what they used to call the "bleeding edge" of technology, finding fun in early adoption and exploration. This perspective on tech has shaped my view on staying current, making this one of my favorite topics to explore. I see technology as more than just useful; it's a gateway to new interests, deeper family connections, and countless ways to enrich our lives. How do you feel about technology? Does it excite or scare you?

Consider recent developments: virtual reality headsets now allow grandparents to play immersive games with their grandchildren across the country; apps like Fitbit and MyFitnessPal make it easy to track and improve physical health from home; or streaming platforms like Masterclass let you take cooking classes or guitar lessons from world-renowned experts—all without leaving your living room.

The Complementary Assets Model: Technology as a Foundation for a Fulfilling Retirement

Earlier in the book, I introduced David Teece's Complementary Assets Model—something I picked up back in business school and, frankly, never expected to dust off in retirement. But the more I reflected, the more it clicked. Retirement isn't one thing—it's a system, just like innovation. Traditionally, the model's used in business, so bear with me while I apply it in a new and admittedly unusual way.

In Chapter 3, we explored how purpose, health, finances, and relationships all work together to bring retirement to life. Now, we're going a level deeper to explore how technology fits into that system and why it only becomes truly valuable when it's surrounded by the right assets to give it meaning, momentum, and, yes, some fun.

Here's the big idea in a nutshell:

Innovation + Assets = Value

A car didn't change the world on its own—it needed roads, gas stations, mechanics, and licenses to become practical. A smartphone? Powerful, but without Wi-Fi, apps, or a cellular network, it's just a sleek gadget with nowhere to go.

In the same way:

Retirement + Technology ≠ Fulfillment

But **Retirement + Technology + the right ecosystem = a rich, connected, purpose-driven life.**

That's the essence of Teece's model. The innovation is powerful, but only when it's paired with the right complementary assets does it change lives.

⬛ What the Tech Ecosystem Looks Like in Retirement

Let's say you have a **Fitbit** (the tech). For it to benefit your health, you also need:

- ✦ **Apps** to track your data (tool)
- ✦ **Motivation** to stay active (habit)
- ✦ **A walking group or workout buddy** (people)
- ✦ **A plan to use the info for better wellness** (purpose)

Together, those create your **tech ecosystem**—a support system that transforms a gadget into a tool for a healthier life.

The Complementary Assets Model in Retirement: Creating a System for Fulfillment

This model perfectly illustrates how a fulfilling retirement, like any innovation, relies on a network of complementary assets. Retirement is a powerful idea—no more work, just time to do what you love. But without essential supports like financial stability, social connection, health, and personal purpose, that freedom can feel unstructured—or even unfulfilling. It's like having a mobile phone with no signal or a car without gas: cool idea, zero functionality.

Here are a few more examples that illustrate the model:

Innovation	Required Complementary Assets
Electric Car	Charging stations, renewable energy sources
Smart Devices	Wi-Fi, apps, cellular network
Air Travel	Airports, air traffic control, baggage systems
Credit Cards	Banking infrastructure, ATMs, merchant terminals
Online Learning	High-speed internet, digital literacy, access to devices
Home Fitness Equipment	Instructional videos, fitness apps, community or coaching support

In our work lives, those supporting pieces were built in—tech training, peer support, daily structure, collaboration. When we retire, that system disappears unless we intentionally build a new one.

Now, we have to create our own ecosystem:

+ Friends or family who keep us updated
+ Online courses or communities that encourage learning
+ Platforms that make tech approachable and relevant
+ Habits and goals that give all that tech a purpose

When those assets come together, tech doesn't just "help" retirement— it supercharges it. Here's how:

Health

You buy a smartwatch. Great. But when paired with health goals, a support system, and daily motivation, that smartwatch becomes a key part of staying active, tracking progress, and maybe even reversing health risks.

Socialization

You join a social media platform. That's nice—but without connection, it's empty. Add in friends, community groups, or shared interests, and it becomes a digital campfire for storytelling, support, and staying in the loop.

Hobbies

You buy a camera. Cool toy. Now add a photo-editing app, a local photography group, and an online portfolio. Suddenly, you're not just taking pictures—you're expressing yourself and building confidence.

Financial

You have a retirement fund. Essential. But paired with complementary assets— diverse income streams, a budget plan, and a part-time gig—it becomes a flexible, secure engine for the lifestyle you want.

Just like retirement requires more than one factor—health, finances, purpose, connection—so does meaningful tech use. Tech alone won't transform your life. But **tech + ecosystem = exponential value.**

So, as you think about your own retirement, ask yourself:

What tools excite me?
What support do I need around them?
How can I build an ecosystem where it all works together?

Because this chapter isn't just about "keeping up." It's about designing your retirement ecosystem—one where innovation actually becomes impact.

This simple visual shows how technology connects to five key assets that power a fulfilling retirement.

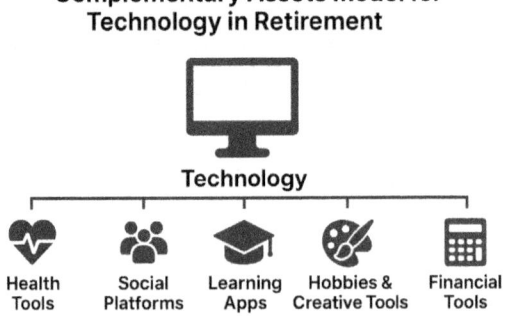

Complementary Assets Model for Technology in Retirement

Technology

Health Tools | Social Platforms | Learning Apps | Hobbies & Creative Tools | Financial Tools

Embracing these complementary assets turns technology from a tool into a gateway for continuous growth, connection, and a sense of purpose in this next stage of life.

Embracing the Tech Revolution: Why Stay Current?

"Do it for Johnny, Man!" - Dally in the movie The Outsiders

Imagine this: You're on a video call with your grandkids, and suddenly they start talking about the latest virtual reality game they're playing. They're zipping through alien worlds or perhaps playing a virtual round of golf, and you're left wondering, "What did I just miss?" In a world that's moving faster than ever, it's easy to feel like the tech train has left the station without you. But it doesn't have to be that way.

Staying current with technology is more than just keeping up - it's about remaining connected, informed, and engaged with the world around you. In retirement, embracing new tech can open doors to exciting new experiences, keep your mind sharp, and even bring you closer to family members who are immersed in the digital world. So, how can we, as retirees, not only keep pace but enjoy the benefits of our tech-driven world?

With so many new technologies emerging daily, you may wonder: why bother? Isn't retirement a time to relax and escape the fast-paced, digital world? While relaxation is vital, staying tech-savvy in retirement can be just as important for overall well-being.

Staying Tech-Savvy: A Growing Trend Among Retirees

Technology use among retirees has surged in recent years. According to Pew Research, 73% of adults aged 65 and older are now online, and over 50% own a smartphone. This age group is the fastest-growing segment of internet users, with many embracing smartphones, tablets, social media, and streaming services.

What's behind the shift? Retirees are discovering how tech supports mental sharpness, social connection, and lifelong learning. From managing finances to exploring new hobbies or simply video chatting with grandchildren, tech is becoming a powerful tool for enriching retirement.

Here's why staying current with tech can be transformative:

1. Boosting Brain Health

Embracing new technologies can stimulate the brain, improving memory, attention span, and problem-solving skills. Engaging with tech provides cognitive benefits comparable to learning a new language or musical instrument.

Research Insight: According to the Global Council on Brain Health, learning new technology helps maintain cognitive function in older adults, encouraging neural plasticity and potentially lowering the risk of cognitive decline.

2. Maintaining Social Connections

Social media and communication tools like FaceTime, WhatsApp, and Zoom allow retirees to stay closely connected with family and friends, offering vital face-to-face interaction regardless of distance.

Research Insight: The University of Michigan found that seniors who use social media report 30% lower rates of loneliness and depression, underscoring the importance of regular social interactions for mental and physical health in retirement.

3. Keeping Up with Family and Friends

Staying tech-savvy bridges the generational gap, allowing retirees to join in on digital activities with younger family members, like texting GIFs, sharing memes, and participating in virtual family events.

Research Insight: Pew Research reveals that 93% of people aged 65+ who use the internet say it improves their ability to stay in touch with family, creating shared digital experiences and new memories with younger generations.

4. Accessing Entertainment and Information

Technology offers endless entertainment and learning opportunities via streaming services, e-books, podcasts, and more. Whether exploring documentaries, novels, or tutorials, tech helps retirees pursue interests effortlessly.

Research Insight: AARP reports that nearly 75% of older adults find digital content enriches their lives, helping them stay informed, engaged, and entertained, which fosters lifelong learning in retirement.

> By staying engaged with technology, you don't just keep up with loved ones but also keep your mind sharp and your spirit invigorated.

Some Technologies to Keep You Engaged in Retirement

Beyond video calls and social media, there are abundant technology tools designed to keep retirees engaged, mentally sharp, and organized. Here are some options to explore:

5. **Online Games for Cognitive Engagement**
    - ✦ **Words with Friends**: Challenge friends worldwide, improving vocabulary and strategic thinking.
    - ✦ **Sudoku Apps**: Apps like *Sudoku.com* and *Brainium Sudoku* offer beginner to expert levels, boosting memory and flexibility.
    - ✦ **Lumosity and Peak**: Brain-training apps that target memory, focus, and flexibility with progress tracking.

6. **Apps for Organizing Retirement Plans**
    - ✦ **Mint**: For budgeting, tracking expenses, and managing investments, helping you stay financially organized.
    - ✦ **Evernote or Google Keep**: Ideal for jotting notes, setting reminders, and organizing daily tasks.
    - ✦ **LastPass**: A secure app for storing and managing passwords, making online account access simpler.

7. **Health-Focused Apps for Wellness Monitoring**
    - ✦ **MyFitnessPal**: Helps track nutrition and exercise to support health goals.
    - ✦ **Apple Health or Google Fit**: Integrates with wearables, offering insights into heart rate, steps, and sleep patterns.
    - ✦ **Pill Reminder by Medisafe**: Tracks multiple prescriptions and sends reminders to help you stay on schedule.

8. **Planning Apps for Future Adventures**
    - ✦ **TripAdvisor or Roadtrippers**: Maps travel plans and locates attractions—ideal for retirees who love exploring.

✦ **BucketListly**: This lets you create and track bucket lists with ideas for activities, places, or hobbies to try.

Integrating these technologies into your retirement can keep you mentally sharp, organized, and engaged, providing a structured and enjoyable experience.

⚠ **Quick heads-up:** *While technology opens up incredible possibilities, it's not all smooth sailing. Be on the lookout for scams, sketchy information, and the occasional rabbit hole that leads to more screen time than soul time. Like anything in retirement, balance is everything.*

Technology in Action: Real-Life Stories of Tech in Retirement

Case Study 1: ChatGPT as a Personal Assistant

John, a 67-year-old retiree, initially thought AI tools like ChatGPT were for tech-savvy millennials. But after his son introduced him to it, he quickly became a fan. Now, John uses ChatGPT to organize his daily schedule, find new recipes, and even write letters to old friends. "It's like having a personal assistant who's always there," he says.

Case Study 2: Virtual Reality for Family Time

Sarah, a 70-year-old grandmother, received an Oculus VR headset as a gift. Skeptical at first, she tried it out by playing a VR game of golf with her grandson and was immediately hooked. Now, they play every week, even though they live miles apart. Sarah notes, "It's brought us closer together."

Case Study 3: A Community Connected by Social Media

Barbara, a 72-year-old retired teacher, felt lonely after her husband passed away, so she joined Facebook. Through Facebook Groups, she discovered local events, rekindled friendships, and joined book clubs. "It has brought a new dimension to my life," she reflects.

Building Your Tech Confidence: Overcoming Tech Terrors

For those less tech-savvy, learning to navigate new technology can feel a lot like Greg's lie detector scene in *Meet the Parents*. Picture this: Greg's father-in-law insists on testing Greg's honesty with an intimidating lie detector, and each beep makes Greg squirm. This humorously captures the discomfort of "high-tech" interactions—especially when you're out of your depth.

Here are a few strategies to build tech confidence:

+ **Start Small**: Try easy-to-use apps, like video calls to connect with family, to build familiarity.
+ **Find a Tech Buddy**: Partnering with a friend or family member makes learning more enjoyable.
+ **Use Online Tutorials**: Many tech tools have step-by-step guides and videos that let you learn at your own pace.

With patience and practice, technology will soon feel like second nature. And remember, each "tech terror" moment is a step closer to mastering the tools that keep you connected and informed.

Embracing technology in retirement opens doors to continued learning, social connections, and enriched well-being. From brain-stimulating games to VR with grandkids and AI assistants, staying tech-savvy enhances daily life in countless ways.

Chapter 9 Takeaways: Staying Current – Adapting to Technology in Retirement

RTF Step 6: Staying Current with the Tools of Modern Life

☑ Technology isn't just about gadgets—it's a gateway to connection, learning, and independence in retirement.

☑ Innovation only creates value when supported by the right system. Retirement + Technology + Ecosystem = Fulfillment.

☑ The Complementary Assets Model shows why tech alone isn't enough—you need people, habits, goals, and support to make it meaningful.

☑ Staying tech-savvy strengthens cognitive health, bridges generational gaps, and empowers you to stay active and informed.

☑ From health tracking and photo sharing to VR golf with grandkids—tech becomes transformative when it's aligned with your life and purpose.

✤ What's Next in the RTF Journey?

In **Chapter 10, Health is Wealth – Prioritizing Physical, Mental, and Spiritual Well-Being**, we'll explore the foundation of a thriving retirement. You can't enjoy your purpose, tech, or passions if your body and mind aren't along for the ride. Let's dive into how to build a healthier, stronger you—inside and out.

Health is Wealth – Prioritizing Physical, Mental, and Spiritual Well-Being

📍 **What you will learn:** Without your health, nothing else in retirement works. Wellness is the ultimate wealth.

Take care of your body. It's the only place you have to live."
— Jim Rohn

How Does Health Connect with Spirituality in Retirement?

Picture yourself at 75, feeling strong, content, and at peace. Your mind is sharp, your body is resilient, and there's a sense of calm that centers you, no matter what comes your way. This isn't just about physical health; your spiritual and emotional well-being play an equally vital role.

What if achieving true health in retirement means finding a balance between body, mind, and spirit? Yes, I am sure you have heard this somewhere before!

In this chapter, we'll dive into how a holistic approach to health can enhance your retirement experience. Part of the Retirement Transition Framework (RTF), this chapter explores ways to stay physically active, proactive about your health, and mentally engaged, encouraging a lifestyle that supports balance and vitality in every aspect of life.

🏋 ♂ Building Strength: Your Physical Foundation

Strength Training, Cardio, and the Power of Flexibility

Strength training is crucial for maintaining muscle mass as we age. Research from the American College of Sports Medicine highlights that adults over 60 should engage in resistance exercises twice a week to counteract muscle loss and improve mobility. Cardio is equally essential; it keeps your heart healthy and provides a natural boost to your mood. According to the Mayo Clinic, regular aerobic exercise can reduce the risk of cardiovascular disease and improve mental health. Pilates, with its focus on core strength and flexibility, is also a fantastic choice to add to your routine, promoting better posture and balance. My wife honestly drug me into a Pilates class a year ago. I was the only guy in the class and had never done Pilates before. I found out 2 things: It's not bad being the only guy in a Pilates class scenery is much better that way! I also found out it focused on the smaller muscles you use for balance and strength and not just big muscles which I had always done. Highly recommend this for people 60+.

Top Recommended Exercises for Those Over 60:

1. **Strength Training:** Bodyweight exercises like squats and resistance band exercises. Pilates offers core strengthening with minimal impact.

2. **Cardio:** Low-impact options like walking, swimming, or dancing.

3. **Flexibility and Balance:** Yoga and Tai Chi improve flexibility and stability, helping prevent falls.

Doctor's Recommendation: "For seniors, regular strength training and cardio exercises not only maintain physical health but also support cognitive function and emotional well-being," says Dr. Maria Nguyen, a geriatric wellness specialist.

Getting Ahead of the Curve: Proactive Health Choices

Being proactive with your health means going beyond routine doctor visits. Retirees now have access to a wide range of resources that can help monitor their well-being outside of traditional medical insurance. Companies like Quest Diagnostics and LabCorp offer consumers the ability to order blood tests directly, providing a comprehensive view of health without needing a doctor's referral. Here's a look at essential screenings that can keep you informed and in control.

Personal Story:

I decided to take my health management into my own hands and ordered a proactive blood test to get a better sense of where I stood. The results weren't alarming at first, but one thing stood out—my cholesterol levels had suddenly spiked. I shared this information with my doctor, which led to him ordering a heart CT scan as a precautionary measure. While they didn't find anything directly related to the cholesterol issue, they did discover something pretty startling: a small aortic aneurysm.

Now, the medical community calls this an "incidental finding," but to me, it didn't sound incidental at all. Aortic aneurysms, though that rare, are often found during testing for other conditions. The key takeaway here was that I would never have known about this without that proactive blood test, and it could have gone undetected for years. The good news is that with routine monitoring and managing my blood pressure, it hasn't grown, and I've been able to manage it effectively. This experience reaffirmed my belief that being proactive about our health, especially in retirement, can uncover things that might otherwise slip through the cracks—and that could make all the difference.

It's stories like mine that emphasize the importance of regular check-ups and screenings. Sometimes, taking that extra step can not only help prevent issues from becoming serious but also uncover hidden risks early on, giving you the tools to stay ahead of potential problems.

Did You Know?

Only about 25% of adults over 65 engage in regular preventive health screenings. By taking proactive steps to monitor your health, you increase your chances of catching potential issues early on, allowing you to address concerns before they become chronic issues.

Essential Routine Tests and Preventive Screenings

Annual Check-Up

1. **Complete Blood Count (CBC):** Helps detect disorders like anemia, infection, and certain cancers by measuring red and white blood cell counts, hemoglobin, and more.

2. **Lipid Panel:** Tracks cholesterol levels (LDL, HDL, triglycerides), a key indicator of heart health. High cholesterol increases the risk for heart disease, so checking annually helps guide dietary and medication choices.

3. **Fasting Blood Glucose or HbA1c:** Essential for tracking blood sugar. An HbA1c test measures glucose levels over the past three months and is useful for identifying or monitoring diabetes.

4. **Thyroid Panel:** Tracks thyroid health (TSH, T3, T4) to monitor metabolic health, as thyroid function can influence energy, mood, and weight.

Every 2-3 Years

1. **Bone Density Test (DEXA scan):** Recommended especially for women over 65 and men over 70 to assess bone health and prevent fractures due to osteoporosis.

2. **Vision and Hearing Tests:** Essential for quality of life and fall prevention as eyes and ears age; advisable every 2-3 years.

Based on Risk Factors

1. **Vitamin D, B12, and Iron Levels:** Important for those at risk for deficiencies, as these affect energy, cognitive function, and immune health.

2. **Cancer Screenings:**
   - **Colonoscopy:** Every 10 years for most adults aged 50-75, more frequently based on family history or findings.
   - **Mammograms or Prostate Screenings:** For women over 50, every two years; for men, discuss PSA testing based on personal risk factors.

3. **Skin Cancer Screening:** An annual skin exam by a dermatologist, especially if there's a history of sun exposure or fair skin.

Convenient At-Home Testing Options At-home testing options from companies like EverlyWell and LetsGetChecked allow you to monitor specific levels of hormones, vitamin D, and even heart health markers without a doctor's visit. For a deeper dive into hereditary conditions, 23andMe and AncestryDNA provide genetic testing to help you make more informed health choices.

Targeted Blood Tests to Monitor Between Annual Visits

If you had high or borderline results in any of your annual screenings, tracking specific blood tests at more frequent intervals can help you manage and adjust as needed. Here's a list of common tests to consider between annual visits, especially if you have known health risks:

1. Lipid Panel

2. Fasting Blood Glucose or HbA1c

3. Liver Function Tests (LFTs)

4. Kidney Function Tests (eGFR and Creatinine)

5. C-Reactive Protein (CRP) or High-Sensitivity CRP (hs-CRP)

6. Thyroid Function Tests (TSH, T3, T4)

7. Vitamin D

8. Iron and Ferritin Levels

9. Electrolytes Panel (Sodium, Potassium, Calcium, Magnesium)

By tracking these blood tests at more frequent intervals, you can adjust early on and avoid letting borderline issues become chronic conditions. These screenings and tests are essential tools for staying on top of your health, allowing you to make informed choices and catch any potential concerns early.

As we work on keeping our bodies in shape, our minds need the same attention to stay sharp and engaged. Retirement offers us the perfect opportunity to focus on cognitive health, just as we prioritize our physical well-being.

🧠 Brainpower Matters: Mental Fitness for Longevity

In addition to physical fitness, maintaining mental agility is essential for a fulfilling retirement. Cognitive exercises, like brain-training apps or learning new skills, help keep the brain active and engaged. Studies have shown that activities such as solving puzzles, learning new languages, or even picking up a musical instrument can reduce the risk of cognitive decline.

Consider these resources for mental engagement:

+ **BrainHQ and Lumosity:** Both platforms offer scientifically backed brain-training exercises designed to improve memory, processing speed, and attention.

- ✦ **Language Learning:** Apps like Duolingo or Babbel allow you to learn a new language, which has been shown to boost cognitive function and delay dementia onset.

- ✦ **Creative Expression:** Exploring art, music, or creative writing stimulates the brain and can bring a sense of joy and accomplishment. Online classes in photography, painting, or even DIY crafts can keep your mind sharp and engaged.

Doctor's Recommendation: "Engaging in mentally stimulating activities is as essential as physical exercise for older adults. Regular cognitive exercise supports brain health and helps prevent age-related memory decline," states Dr. James Patel, neurologist and aging specialist.

🕉 Finding Purpose: Spiritual Resilience in Retirement

Just as physical and mental health contribute to a fulfilling retirement, spiritual well-being plays an essential role. Whether rooted in religious practices or personal reflection, spirituality offers us resilience and a deeper sense of purpose. Many retirees find that exploring their spiritual beliefs helps them handle life's challenges with grace, strength, and inner peace.

Research Insight: According to the National Institute on Aging, seniors who engage in spiritual practices or community-based faith activities experience lower stress and depression levels, with a stronger sense of life satisfaction.

Spiritual health is an essential part of well-being in retirement. Whether it's rooted in religious practices or personal reflection, spirituality gives us a deeper sense of purpose and helps us develop resilience to face life's challenges. Many retirees find that exploring their spiritual beliefs brings inner peace and a stronger sense of life satisfaction.

Personal Story:

Years ago, I used to attend church regularly, but eventually, I found myself drifting away. I think a big part of it was that the church I attended didn't resonate with me—it felt outdated, and the teachings didn't seem to offer much relevance for today's world. It wasn't that I had lost my faith; it was just that the church wasn't speaking to me in a way that was meaningful.

However, when Suzanne and I moved to a new state, we found a church that felt completely different. A friend of my parents used to call these types of churches "alive"—and I can see why. This new church was vibrant, modern, and the teachings were so much more relatable. They weren't just presenting ancient scriptures; they were offering ways to live by them in today's world.

What I found most striking was how much this spiritual growth has become a cornerstone of my retirement system. It's given me a new sense of purpose and connection, helping me navigate the changes that come with retirement. Spiritual health, for me, has been just as crucial as physical health. It's about grounding yourself in something greater than just the everyday routines and challenges— something that adds meaning to everything you do.

Just as spirituality grounds us in a deeper purpose, the food we eat nourishes and fuels our bodies, providing us with the energy to engage in every aspect of life. Much like how a spiritual practice contributes to mental and emotional health, the right diet can be foundational for maintaining physical well-being and giving us the strength to live our purpose. Let's now acknowledge the role diet plays in our holistic health, ensuring we maintain balance in both mind and body.

🍎 Fueling the Body: Nutrition for Energy and Longevity

No discussion on health would be complete without mentioning diet—after all, it's a vital part of our overall well-being. While this chapter won't dive into specific diets, a few simple principles can make a significant difference:

+ **Prioritize Whole Foods**: Focus on incorporating more whole foods like fruits, vegetables, whole grains, lean proteins, and healthy fats. They're packed with nutrients and help maintain steady energy throughout the day.

+ **Stay Hydrated:** Drinking enough water is crucial for almost every bodily function. Aim for at least eight glasses a day, or more if you're active. Try to make water your main beverage, limiting sugary drinks.

+ **Practice Portion Control:** Eating balanced portions helps avoid overeating and keeps you feeling energized rather than sluggish. Using smaller plates and listening to hunger cues can be great tools for portion management.

These small, manageable habits can make a world of difference, enhancing both physical vitality and mental clarity. For more detailed guidance, explore resources that resonate with your personal goals and consult your healthcare provider to align your diet with any specific health needs.

Now that we've covered the key areas of health—physical activity, mental wellness, spirituality, and nutrition—it's time to put it all together with actionable steps that will support your holistic well-being in retirement. Let's now look at some practical steps to make this balance a reality in your daily life. Next, let's put it all together with actionable steps that support a holistic approach to health, ensuring each day is enriched with purpose, energy, and resilience. With that, let's move on to a holistic step to health.

☑️ Weekly Playbook: Putting Your Health Plan Into Action

The following steps provide practical strategies to enhance each area of your well-being. Designed to be actionable and easy to implement, these suggestions can help you build routines that support a fulfilling and balanced retirement journey.

(Just a Starting Point — Make It Yours!)

Here's a simple way to bring your health goals to life each week. Nothing fancy—just a way to stay on track and feel accomplished without needing a whiteboard, a stopwatch, or a personal trainer named Mike yelling "Push harder!" at you.

📝 Sample Weekly Health Plan Template (Customize to Fit Your Goals)

Focus Area	Goal	Sample Activities	Completed? ✅
Strength Training	2x/week	Resistance bands, squats, Pilates	[ ] [ ]
Cardio	150 mins/week (30x5)	Walk, swim, cycle, dance	[ ] [ ] [ ] [ ] [ ]
Flexibility	2x/week	Yoga, Tai Chi	[ ] [ ]
Cognitive Health	10 min/day	Brain app, new hobby	M T W T F S S
Mindfulness	5–10 min/day	Calm app, breathing	M T W T F S S
Spiritual/Community	1–2x/month	Church, study group, meditation	[ ] [ ]

💡 **Pro tip**: Put this somewhere visible—a fridge, bathroom mirror, or next to your morning coffee setup. Checking those boxes might be the most satisfying thing you do all week (besides finishing a good Netflix series).

1. Set a Weekly Fitness Routine

Rocky's Iconic Training Montage – Strength and Endurance Building

In *Rocky*, we see Rocky Balboa pushing his limits through intense training (and eating raw eggs for breakfast!), sprinting up steps, punching bags, and focusing on building strength and resilience. His dedication to cardio and strength training gives him the stamina he needs to face his toughest challenges.

Just as Rocky's training builds his endurance and resilience, incorporating cardio and strength exercises into your routine can maintain energy, heart health, and muscle tone. To be clear, I am not suggesting you train like Rocky! Let's dive into exercises that can keep you physically fit and feeling strong in retirement.

✦ **Strength Training:**
- **Goal:** Include two days a week of resistance exercises to maintain muscle mass and bone density.
- **Suggestions:** Start with bodyweight exercises like squats, lunges, and push-ups. Progress with resistance bands or light weights.
- **Tip:** Consider senior-focused strength classes offered at community centers for a safe environment to learn proper form and technique.
- **Tool:** Use a fitness tracking app like MyFitnessPal or Fitbit to log your workouts and track progress over time.

✦ **Cardio:**
- **Goal:** Aim for at least 150 minutes of moderate cardio per week, broken into manageable sessions (e.g., 30 minutes, five times a week).
- **Suggestions:** Walking, swimming, or cycling are low-impact options that support cardiovascular health. Try dancing classes, which also help with coordination and balance.

- ◆ **Tip:** If joint health is a concern, swimming or water aerobics offers a low-impact, effective cardio workout.
- ◆ **Tool:** Try an app like Map My Run or Strava to track your walks, bike rides, or swims, and keep yourself motivated.

✦ **Flexibility and Balance:**
- ◆ **Goal:** Dedicate at least two sessions per week to flexibility and balance exercises.
- ◆ **Suggestions:** Yoga and Tai Chi help improve balance, coordination, and range of motion. Consider trying Pilates for core strength.
- ◆ **Tip:** Explore online videos or local classes to find a style that suits your fitness level and interests.
- ◆ **Tool:** Yoga Studio or Glo are great apps for guided sessions on yoga, Tai Chi, and Pilates at your own pace.

2. **Schedule a Comprehensive Health Check-Up**

**The Lord of the Rings Fellowship Formation
– Preparing for the Journey Ahead**

In *The Lord of the Rings: The Fellowship of the Ring*, each member of the fellowship prepares, both physically and mentally, for the long journey ahead. The goal is simple: be ready for anything that lies ahead by covering all bases in advance.

Much like the fellowship preparing themselves for the trials ahead, a regular health check-up is key to navigating retirement's health landscape. Personally, I am a big believer in managing and tracking your health with your doctor to include typical checkups but also going beyond what the insurance industry thinks is best for your health, if you have the time and resources.

✦ **Routine Tests and Preventive Screenings:**
- ◆ **Goal:** Plan an annual check-up with blood tests, hormone pancls, vitamin assessments, and cardiovascular screenings.
- ◆ **Suggestions:** Investigate Quest Diagnostics or LabCorp for accessible blood tests outside of insurance and consider Lifeline Screening for vascular health checks.

- **Tip:** Use a health tracking app like Apple Health or Google Fit to store and monitor your test results, making it easier to track changes over time.

✦ **Regular Check-Ins:**
- **Goal:** Every quarter, review key health metrics and adjust lifestyle habits as needed.
- **Suggestions:** Track at-home blood pressure readings, and review these with your healthcare provider to maintain proactive health management.
- **Tip:** Use an app like Withings or Omron to monitor your blood pressure or other vital signs, ensuring they stay within healthy ranges.

3. Engage in Cognitive Health Activities

Wax On, Wax Off: Mental Training in Retirement

In *The Karate Kid*, Mr. Miyagi's "wax on, wax off" lesson starts as a seemingly mundane chore but turns out to be a transformative training method, equipping young Daniel with skills he didn't know he was developing. Daniel was frustrated (I would have been, too!) until he understood the genius behind Mr. Miyagi's plan. It's a powerful reminder that sometimes the repetitive tasks we don't fully understand can build strength, resilience, and skill over time.

Daily mental exercises, like solving puzzles or learning something new, can feel repetitive, but they strengthen cognitive abilities over time. Just as Daniel sees the purpose behind Mr. Miyagi's lesson, these small daily activities build a foundation for mental agility.

✦ **Brain Training:**
- **Goal:** Spend at least 10 minutes a day on brain exercises.
- **Suggestions:** Try apps like BrainHQ or Lumosity to work on memory and processing speed.
- **Tip:** Treat it like a daily habit, like exercise, to keep your brain engaged and active.

+ **Creative Pursuits:**

  o **Goal:** Dedicate time weekly to hobbies or new skills that stimulate the mind.

  o **Suggestions:** Enroll in online art or music classes or pick up a craft you've always wanted to try.

  o **Tip:** Learning something new boosts cognitive health and keeps you engaged in a fun, fulfilling way.

  o **Tool:** Use Skillshare or Masterclass to explore new creative pursuits, whether it's painting, photography, or even learning to play an instrument.

4. **Explore Mindfulness and Meditation**

Yoda's Jedi Training – Focus and Inner Calm

In *The Empire Strikes Back*, Yoda teaches Luke to focus and tap into his inner strength through calm and patience. Through his guidance, Luke learns that inner peace and focus can be powerful tools when facing life's challenges. "Luke, I am your father!" Sorry, I was just dying to say that.

Much like Yoda's meditation practices teach Luke to center his mind, mindfulness and meditation can help you build resilience and peace in retirement. Let's explore simple mindfulness exercises that cultivate inner calm and boost emotional well-being.

+ **Mindfulness and Meditation:**
  - **Goal:** Dedicate 5-10 minutes daily to meditation, gradually increasing as you get comfortable.
  - **Suggestions:** Try apps like Headspace or Calm, which offer guided sessions focused on breathing, mindfulness, and relaxation.
  - **Tip:** Meditate at the same time each day to build a consistent habit that enhances emotional resilience.

5. **Join a Spiritual or Community Group**

Remember the Titans' Team Building – Finding Unity in Community

In *Remember the Titans*, a team of young athletes learns, after some tough times, the power of unity and community support. Through team-building exercises, they find strength in their differences and become a cohesive unit that's stronger together.

Just as the Titans learned the value of team unity, finding a supportive community or spiritual group can enrich your retirement experience. Let's look at how joining community groups can foster purpose, belonging, and connection.

✦ **Research and Attend Gatherings:**
  - **Goal:** Attend one gathering or service per month to explore different spiritual or community groups.
  - **Suggestions:** Look for churches, meditation centers, or virtual communities that align with your beliefs and values.
  - **Tip:** Sample different groups to find one where you feel welcome and inspired to engage further.

✦ **Engage with Group Activities:**
  - **Goal:** Participate in one group activity outside regular services, such as study groups, volunteer events, or community outings.
  - **Suggestions:** Many communities offer workshops or discussions that create deeper connections and shared experiences.
  - **Tip:** Building camaraderie and a sense of belonging can enrich your social and spiritual journey in retirement.

⚠ Before You Begin: A Note on Health Choices

The information in this chapter is designed to provide helpful insights into maintaining your health in retirement, but remember, everyone's needs are unique.

☑ **Always consult your primary care physician** before:

✦ Starting a new exercise program

✦ Ordering independent health tests

✦ Making significant changes to your nutrition or supplement routine

Sharing results from at-home or self-ordered tests with your doctor ensures they become part of your overall health record—and that you receive the best possible guidance for your long-term well-being.

Health in Retirement: Building a Foundation for Lifelong Well-Being

Health in retirement is about finding a balance that works for you—one that nurtures your body, mind, and spirit without being overly rigid or restrictive. By incorporating regular exercise, proactive health screenings, mental engagement, and moments of reflection or connection, you can cultivate a fulfilling and vibrant retirement. This journey is yours to shape, so take the flexibility of retirement as a chance to discover what truly enhances your well-being.

When you prioritize physical health, nurture your mental wellness, and proactively manage your well-being, you're building a strong foundation for the rest of your retirement. These steps are essential within the Retirement Transition Framework (RTF), helping you stay resilient, adaptable, and full of life as you navigate change.

With a firm grasp on how health can shape a fulfilling retirement, it's time to bring everything together. In the final chapter, *The Retirement Transition Framework (RTF) in Action: My Plan for a Fulfilling Retirement*, we'll dive into how I applied the RTF to design my own retirement journey. Through personal stories and real-life examples, I hope to inspire you to craft a retirement plan that resonates with your values and aspirations, guiding you toward a life filled with purpose, growth, and satisfaction.

The Retirement Transition Framework (RTF) in Action

What you will learn: Reinvention is possible, with a plan. The RTF helps you turn reflection into action and live with purpose

"You are never too old to set another goal or to dream a new dream."
— *C.S. Lewis*

My Personal Journey Through the RTF

When I first stepped into retirement, I felt like a ship adrift at sea—no compass, no clear direction, just endless time and no playbook. After years of structure, deadlines, and purpose, I suddenly had all the freedom I thought I wanted... and none of the clarity I needed.

That's when I created the Retirement Transition Framework (RTF). Honestly, it was part survival instinct, part business-school reflex. After all, my Oxford classmates would've given me grief if I didn't build some kind of model! But more importantly, I needed a structure—not to tell me what to do, but to help me figure out what mattered now.

The RTF didn't magically fix everything. What it did was get me asking better questions. It gave me something to work with when everything else felt up in the air.

At first, the steps just gave me momentum. I started writing—something I'd never considered seriously before. That small experiment turned into a full-blown passion and, ultimately, this book.

I also found myself drawn to volunteering in a way I hadn't expected—particularly the kind that let me contribute during real moments of crisis. That work filled a need in me I didn't even realize I had. It was hands-on, real-time, and it gave me back the sense of usefulness and urgency I'd lost when I stepped away from my career.

I began being more intentional with family, with friends, and with my health. I took the time to rewire—not just retire. The framework didn't hand me a brand-new life on a silver platter. But it helped me build one, brick by brick, based on what really matters.

So, who am I now in retirement?

I'm a writer. A purposeful volunteer. A connector with my family. A health-focused version of my old self. A better friend. And someone who's still figuring it out—on purpose, and with direction.

Other Examples of the RTF in Action

Let's take a look at how the RTF worked for others. Each person's journey was unique, but the framework helped them define their own path toward fulfillment.

Sarah's Transformation: From Corporate Leader to Financial Literacy Advocate

Sarah spent 35 years as a high-level financial executive—boardrooms, spreadsheets, and pressure-filled meetings were her daily rhythm. When she retired, she welcomed the slower pace... at first. But it didn't take long before the novelty wore off and something deeper surfaced: "I miss being needed," she told me.

That's when she returned to the RTF and started asking herself some tough questions: What parts of my job brought me the most energy? What can I do with that now? Turns out, Sarah's real passion was helping people understand money—not for profits, but for life.

She started volunteering to teach basic financial literacy in her community, from young adults navigating credit for the first time to seniors worried about fixed incomes. Before long, she was leading monthly workshops and even pursued a certification in financial education. Today, Sarah says, "I feel more useful than I did in my career. I may not be running a company, but I'm still making a difference."

Tom's Journey: From Construction Manager to Outdoor Enthusiast and Mentor

Tom worked in construction for over four decades. He was the guy who got up before dawn, ran job sites, and mentored the younger guys coming up. Retirement, for him, sounded like bliss. No more deadlines. No more jobsite stress.

But a few months in, he felt... unanchored. "I didn't miss the work," he said, "but I missed having a crew." That's where the RTF helped. Tom realized that what he really loved wasn't pouring concrete—it was helping people grow.

So, he combined that with something else he loved: the outdoors. Tom started volunteering with a local youth group, organizing hiking trips and teaching basic carpentry. Then he launched a small mentorship program for at-risk teens, giving them real skills and a sense of direction.

He's still got his early mornings, but now they're on the trail, not the jobsite. "The RTF didn't just give me a plan," Tom told me. "It helped me see that the best parts of me weren't tied to a paycheck."

Bob's Journey: From Sales Veteran to Wellness Advocate

Bob was a legend in sales—40 years of beating quotas, building relationships, and closing deals. Retirement looked like the finish line he'd earned. But when the calls stopped and his calendar went blank, he admitted something most people don't: "I had no clue who I was without the hustle."

The RTF helped Bob get honest about what he had been ignoring: his health. All those years on the road, fast food lunches, long hours—it had taken a toll. Instead of jumping into a new job or side hustle, he leaned into something more personal.

He started walking. Then running. Then reading about nutrition. Before long, he was hosting neighborhood wellness walks and inviting local experts to give talks on heart health and stress reduction. The best part? He wasn't doing it for a commission. He was doing it because it felt good.

Bob now calls himself a "reluctant health nut." But he also says, "I feel better at 65 than I did at 50—and I'm finally giving back in a way that doesn't feel like a transaction."

Ellen's Journey: From Public School Teacher to Mindful Explorer of Life

Ellen didn't want a second act. After 40 years in the classroom, what she craved wasn't activity—it was stillness. But when she finally got it, the silence felt strange. "Without my classroom, I wasn't sure who I was," she said quietly.

She didn't want to lead a nonprofit or become a travel blogger. Instead, the RTF gave her permission to explore something else entirely: doing less, but with more meaning. She created a gentle rhythm—mornings with coffee and a journal, long walks under the trees, reading a new book each month, and attending a contemplative prayer group.

"I didn't need to fill my days—I needed to feel them," she told me one afternoon. "The RTF helped me see that growth doesn't always have to be loud. Sometimes, it's just learning to be still and okay with who you are now."

Her story reminds us that not every retirement transformation has to be flashy. Some of the most profound reinventions happen quietly, one mindful breath at a time.

Taking Your Time: Transition at Your Own Pace

It's natural to feel energized after developing your RTF plan. You've got direction, excitement, and a sense of purpose—but remember, this is a transition. It's okay to take things at your own pace. There's no rush to achieve everything at once, and it's important to allow yourself time to adjust to this new chapter.

Dr. Nancy Schlossberg, a psychologist who has studied life transitions, reminds us, "Retirement is not just a financial decision; it's a psychological journey. Take your time, lean into the change, and allow yourself to transition at your own speed."

You're creating a life filled with purpose and meaning—there's no need to sprint through it. Enjoy the process, be patient with yourself, and know that it's okay if things unfold gradually.

Because when the time comes to step up and design your next chapter, just like I once had to in a surprising place, you'll be more ready than you think.

You may not expect life to hand you a final exam in retirement—but when it does, you'll be more prepared than you think. I learned that lesson in an unexpected place—one that became a perfect metaphor for the RTF in action.

One Last Story for You

Looking back, I can't help but think of my time at Oxford, where my cohort and I faced an exam experience that pushed our limits in every way. Picture this: we weren't a group of 20-somethings—nope, we were seasoned executives, ages 38 to 55, fresh out of an intense term, handed a business case to prep for each exam. They didn't give us any hints about what questions would hit us; we just knew we had to be ready for anything.

On exam day, we'd file into this ancient, almost intimidating building, a place so drenched in tradition it felt like stepping into another world. No modern tech, no innovation—just history and ritual. And the dress code? Enter *sub-fusc*, this traditional academic dress that included a gown, cap, and strict guidelines down to the color of your socks. Miss one detail? You're out. It was Seinfeld's "Soup Nazi" but on a whole other level: "No exam for you!"

And it didn't stop there. Professors were out of the picture; instead, a group of serious proctors managed the whole process. They'd guide us to our desks in a vast hall, walls lined with oil portraits of alumni who looked like they belonged in a historical drama. And there we'd sit, each of us identified only by a number, like some academic spy game. Honestly, I'd never experienced anything like it—a setting that intense, with an air of mystery and tradition that's hard to describe.

Then came the exam booklets. Two hours on the clock, and nothing but a pen in hand. When we flipped those booklets open, it was go-time. These weren't "tell us what you know" questions; they were more like, "Imagine you're consulting for Google—what's your move? Now, write a memo to the CEO." Two hours of all-out sprinting to capture everything we'd learned—insights, frameworks, strategies, everything we'd absorbed. By the end, every single one of us was wiped out but strangely satisfied.

That experience taught me something powerful about putting knowledge into real-world action—and in a funny way, it's exactly what the Retirement Transition Framework (RTF) is here to do.

I'm not just sharing this as a story about Oxford; it's a metaphor for retirement itself. It's like staring down a blank exam booklet, an open page where you get to decide what comes next. Retirement asks us to pause, reflect, and design a new plan for ourselves. This is your chance to take everything you've learned—your values, your experiences, your vision—and map out something that's uniquely yours.

Final Thoughts – Celebrating Your Journey and Embracing the Future

As you close this book, let's take a moment to reflect on the journey we've taken here together. Retirement brings both freedom and unexpected challenges, and sharing my story was one way to help others realize they're not alone in figuring it all out.

Throughout these pages, I shared a mix of insights, personal stories, and a little humor, all to make what can be a serious and even overwhelming topic feel a bit lighter and more relatable. Now, let's look back at the main steps of the Retirement Transition Framework (RTF) and how they can tie together to help you design a fulfilling retirement. Here's a look at each step and how it came to life throughout the book.

1. Transitioning from Career to Retirement

We started with the emotional and mental shift from career to retirement. Leaving behind a structured, purpose-driven work life can feel like stepping into unknown territory. Acknowledging that initial shock, the RTF helps you turn the page and prepare for this new chapter by asking the right questions about what you want this phase of life to mean.

2. Managing Your Finances

Financial stability is the foundation of any successful retirement. Without a clear financial plan, it's hard to fully embrace your new purpose or explore new passions. In this step, the RTF encourages you to create a robust financial plan, helping you feel secure and ready to engage in everything else retirement offers.

3. Beyond Financial Planning

This step is all about purpose. Financial security alone isn't enough for a meaningful retirement. In this chapter, we focused on the essential need for purpose—whether that's community involvement, family, or personal projects that keep you motivated and fulfilled.

4. Embracing Change and Redefining Success

Retirement isn't just an end; it's a chance to redefine what success looks like for you. Letting go of career-based metrics of success is freeing but takes work. Here, the RTF helps you develop a mindset of growth and openness to change, setting you up to fully enjoy and embrace this chapter.

5. Exploring New Passions

Without the daily demands of a job, you finally have the time to explore new interests. The RTF encourages you to dive into your curiosities, discovering hobbies, skills, and interests that can add a new layer of excitement to your life.

6. Strengthening Relationships

Retirement can be isolating if we're not intentional about maintaining and building relationships. In this step, the RTF emphasizes the importance of nurturing connections with family, friends, and communities, reinforcing the value of a socially engaged retirement.

7. Leaving a Legacy

Many of us hope to leave something meaningful behind. Here, the RTF guides you to consider how you want to impact your family, community, or even just the people closest to you. Creating a legacy can add lasting purpose and fulfillment.

8. Staying Current with Technology

Technology isn't just for the young! The RTF highlights the importance of staying connected with the modern world, using digital tools for learning, community, and entertainment. Embracing technology can help you feel engaged, connected, and empowered in a world that's always changing.

9. Prioritizing Health – Physical, Mental, and Spiritual

Health is the cornerstone of enjoying all that retirement has to offer. In this step, we talked about the benefits of physical exercise, mental wellness practices, and spiritual exploration. The RTF encourages a holistic approach to health so that you're in top shape to live your life fully.

10. Putting It All Together

The RTF is not a one-size-fits-all checklist but a flexible guide for you to design a retirement that feels right for you. Like my Oxford exam experience, it's all about taking what you've learned, thinking deeply about your values and goals, and crafting a personal "case study" for your life.

📋 RTF at a Glance: Your 10-Step Framework

RTF Snapshot: Your Retirement Roadmap

RTF Step	Core Focus	Key Question
1. Career to Retirement	Emotional & identity shift	Who am I without my job?
2. Financial Foundation	Stability as the launchpad	Can I build purpose on this foundation?
3. Purpose	Beyond the numbers	What gives me meaning now?
4. Embracing Change	Letting go of the old you	What am I ready to release or explore?
5. Exploring Passions	Curiosity and fulfillment	What lights me up inside?
6. Relationships	Social and family connections	Who matters most, and how do I show up?
7. Legacy	Impact beyond yourself	What do I want to leave behind?
8. Technology	Staying relevant and connected	Am I open to learning and evolving?
9. Health	Wellness in body, mind, and spirit	How can I take better care of myself?

Chapter 11 Takeaways: The RTF in Action – Living With Purpose

☑ The Retirement Transition Framework (RTF) isn't theoretical—it's a practical tool for designing a fulfilling retirement, one step at a time.

☑ Your journey through the RTF doesn't have to be fast or flashy growth can be quiet, gradual, and deeply personal.

☑ Real-life stories show that fulfillment can come from service, creativity, stillness, or reinvention—there's no one-size-fits-all.

☑ You're not starting over; you're building forward, using your values and life experience as the foundation.

☑ Like any exam worth taking, retirement invites reflection, preparation, and purpose. The RTF is your guidebook—not a rulebook—for what's next.

The RTF helped me transform my retirement, and my hope is that it gives you the same clarity, purpose, and fulfillment in your journey.

This is your next adventure, and you deserve to thrive in it. We've all worked hard to retire, and damn it, we deserve to enjoy it! We deserve not just to live but to thrive - with excitement, happiness, and purpose. So, as Fleetwood Mac would say, "Don't stop thinking about tomorrow." Embrace the future with excitement and confidence - it's going to be an incredible ride!

Retirement isn't the end of the story—it's your plot twist. And you're the author now!

Acknowledgments

Writing this book has been a deeply personal journey, and I'm incredibly grateful to the many people, tools, and resources that helped bring it to life.

First, I would like to thank Jim McLaughlin for his thoughtful advice, editorial insights, and willingness to challenge ideas to make them stronger. Your input helped elevate this book.

To Tara Griffin, thank you for providing blunt feedback on the book idea, summary, title, and cover design—your candor helped push the marketing in the right direction.

I also want to thank Tariq Khan for his expert work on the book's layout and formatting.

To my family, thank you for your patience, support, and encouragement throughout this process. Your belief in me gave this project its heartbeat.

Research and Book Development Methodology

Use of Generative AI Tools

Generative AI tools, including ChatGPT (OpenAI) and Meta AI, were used to assist with grammar editing, word-smithing, clarifying ideas, and refining structure, similar in function to how some authors use ghostwriters or editors to polish their work. These tools helped improve the flow and readability of the content without compromising the author's original ideas, concepts, or voice.

Digital Research Resources

In addition to AI tools, internet-based platforms such as Google, Safari, and other search engines were used to locate expert quotes, up-to-date statistics, and relevant reference works, particularly in the areas of psychology, retirement planning, and behavioral science.

Academic Influence

Insights drawn from academic research, strategic frameworks, and expert perspectives helped shape some sections of this book. Some of these ideas were informed by materials studied during my time at Oxford University, particularly around strategy, corporate innovation, leadership, and personal reinvention.

Public Library Resources

Special thanks to the Gulf Gate Public Library, Sarasota, Florida, whose public reference tools and librarian support were valuable in fact-checking and content enrichment.

Appendix: Resources and References

Academic Citations.

+ **American College of Sports Medicine. (n.d.).** Exercise and Physical Activity for Older Adults. American College of Sports Medicine.

+ **American Psychological Association.** (n.d.). *Research on family connections and emotional health in retirement.*

+ **BlackPast.** (n.d.). *Oseola McCarty (1908–1999).* Retrieved from https://www.blackpast.org/african-american-history/oseola-mccarty-1908-1999/

+ **Brown, B.** (2012). *Daring Greatly.* Gotham Books.

+ **Brown, Dr. Stuart.** (2009). *Play: How It Shapes the Brain, Opens the Imagination, and Invigorates the Soul.* Avery.

+ **Doidge, N.** (2007). *The Brain That Changes Itself: Stories of Personal Triumph from the Frontiers of Brain Science.* Penguin Books.

+ **Gibson, W.** (2003, December 4). *"The future is here; it's just unevenly distributed."* The Economist.

+ **Global Council on Brain Health.** (n.d.). *Research on cognitive benefits of learning new technology for older adults.*

+ **Holt-Lunstad, J.** (n.d.). *Research on social bonds and life expectancy.*

+ **Institute of Economic Affairs (2013)** – for the 40% increased risk of depression in retirement

+ **Insured Retirement Institute.** (n.d.). *Survey on baby boomers' retirement savings.*

+ **Jackson, P.** (Director). (2001). *The Lord of the Rings: The Fellowship of the Ring* [Film]. New Line Cinema.

✦ **Journal of Happiness Studies.** (n.d.). *Research insights on mental health challenges among retirees.*

✦ **Journal of Positive Psychology.** (n.d.). *Study on life satisfaction among retirees who pursue hobbies.*

✦ **Journal of Psychology and Aging.** (2019). *Study on identity loss in retirement.*

✦ **Levin, B. B.** (n.d.). *Quote on work providing social connections, structure, and contribution. General reference from her work as a gerontologist.*

✦ **Leider, R. J.** (2015). *The Power of Purpose: Find Meaning, Live Longer, Better.* Berrett-Koehler Publishers.

✦ **Mayo Clinic.** (n.d.). *Aerobic exercise: How to warm up and cool down.* Retrieved from mayoclinic.org.

✦ **McCarty, O.** (n.d.). *Quote and legacy of philanthropy in education.*

✦ **Merrill Lynch.** (n.d.). *Survey on legacy desires among retirees.*

✦ **Musk, E.** (n.d.). *Quote on meaning derived from employment.* Source: interview or article.

✦ **National Institute on Aging.** (n.d.). *Research on spirituality and life satisfaction in older adults.* Retrieved from nia.nih.gov.

✦ **Nguyen, M.** (Fictitious name). *Quote on seniors' physical and cognitive health. (Note: Replace with real expert or clearly indicate as fictional).*

✦ **Pew Research Center.** (n.d.). *Survey on technology usage trends among adults 65+.*

✦ **Pressfield, S.** (2002). *The War of Art: Break Through the Blocks and Win Your Inner Creative Battles.* Black Irish Entertainment.

✦ **Psychological Science** – for the emotional well-being and purpose findings.

✦ **Psychological Science Journal.** (n.d.). *Study on life satisfaction and legacy among older adults.*

✦ **Reznik, Dr. Amy.** (n.d.). *Embracing technology that aligns with personal interests.* General gerontology recommendation.

✦ **Robbins, T.** (2014). *Money: Master the Game.* Simon & Schuster.

✦ **Rohr, R.** (2011). *Falling Upward: A Spirituality for the Two Halves of Life.* Jossey-Bass.

- **Rosen, Dr. Larry D.** (2016). *The Distracted Mind: Ancient Brains in a High-Tech World,* co-authored with Adam Gazzaley. MIT Press.

- **Ryff, C. D.** (1989). *Happiness is everything, or is it? Explorations on the meaning of psychological well-being.* Journal of Personality and Social Psychology, 57(6), 1069–1081.

- **Schlossberg, N. K.** (2004). *Retire Smart, Retire Happy: Finding Your True Path in Life.* American Psychological Association.

- **Small, Dr. Gary.** (2008). *iBrain: Surviving the Technological Alteration of the Modern Mind.* HarperCollins.

- **Teece, D.** (n.d.). *Complementary Assets Model. Strategic model for value creation.*

- **University of Michigan.** (n.d.). *Research on social media's impact on loneliness in seniors.*

- **Whitbourne, S. K.** (n.d.). *Quote on letting go and retirement transitions. General reference for life transitions.*

Media Citations.

- **A Christmas Carol.** (1843). Dickens, C. [Novel].

- **Dead Poets Society.** (1989). Weir, P. (Director). Touchstone Pictures.

- **Ferris Bueller's Day Off.** (1986). Hughes, J. (Director). Paramount Pictures.

- **Fleetwood Mac.** (1977). *Don't Stop.* On *Rumours* [Album]. Warner Bros. Records.

- **Going in Style.** (2017). Braff, Z. (Director). Warner Bros.

- **The Bucket List.** (2007). Reiner, R. (Director). Warner Bros.

- **The Lord of the Rings:** The Fellowship of the Ring. (2001). Directed by P. Jackson. New Line Cinema.

- **The Outsiders.** (1983). Coppola, F. F. (Director). Warner Bros., based on the novel by S.E. Hinton.

- **Office Space.** (1999). Judge, M. (Director). 20th Century Fox.

- **Remember the Titans.** (2000). Yakin, B. (Director). Walt Disney Pictures.

- ✦ **Rocky**. (1976). Stallone, S. (Writer), & Avildsen, J. G. (Director). United Artists.
- ✦ **Rocky Balboa**. (2006). Stallone, S. (Writer & Director).
- ✦ **Star Wars:** The Empire Strikes Back. (1980). Directed by I. Kershner. Lucasfilm.

Institutional References.

- ✦ **Carter Center** – A nonprofit founded by Jimmy Carter, focused on human rights, public health, and conflict resolution, with initiatives in disease eradication and democratic governance.
- ✦ **Centers for Disease Control and Prevention (CDC)** – The U.S. public health agency responsible for disease prevention, health education, and response to health threats.
- ✦ **Department of Health and Human Services (HHS)** – The U.S. federal agency focused on protecting public health and providing essential health and social services.
- ✦ **Department of Homeland Security (DHS)** – The U.S. department dedicated to safeguarding the nation from threats, including terrorism, cyber-attacks, and natural disasters.
- ✦ **Employee Benefit Research Institute (EBRI)** – A research organization providing data on retirement security, analyzing retirees' savings and financial challenges to support policy and financial planning.
- ✦ **Eva Perón Foundation** – An Argentine foundation dedicated to social welfare, providing healthcare, education, and housing support for underprivileged communities, inspired by Eva Perón's humanitarian vision.
- ✦ **Labcorp (Laboratory Corporation of America Holdings)** – A global life sciences company offering diagnostic testing and drug development services to improve health and advance scientific research.
- ✦ **The Pentagon** – The main headquarters of the U.S. Department of Defense, overseeing national defense and military operations.

- ✦ **Quest Diagnostics – Quest** Offers diagnostic testing services, including over 75 tests through QuestDirect™, enabling consumers to manage their health independently.

- ✦ **Social Security Administration (SSA)** – The U.S. agency that administers social security benefits, including retirement, disability, and survivor benefits.

Referenced Technologies and Apps

- ✦ **23andMe** – A genetic testing service offering insights into ancestry, health traits, and wellness.

- ✦ **Airbnb** – A popular platform that allows homeowners to rent out spare rooms or entire properties to travelers, providing a flexible way to generate extra income with short-term stays.

- ✦ **AR Headsets** – Wearable devices that use augmented reality to overlay digital elements onto the real world for interactive experiences.

- ✦ **Babbel** – A language-learning app focused on developing conversational language skills through interactive lessons.

- ✦ **BucketListly** – An app designed for creating, organizing, and tracking personal bucket list goals.

- ✦ **Calm** – A meditation and relaxation app that promotes mental well-being through guided meditation, sleep aids, and mindfulness practices.

- ✦ **Coursera** – An online platform that provides access to courses, specializations, and degrees from leading universities and institutions.

- ✦ **edX** – An online learning platform offering university-level courses, professional certificates, and programs from global institutions.

- ✦ **Etsy** – An online marketplace where individuals can buy and sell handmade, vintage, and unique items, popular among crafters and retirees.

- ✦ **Fitbit** – A wearable fitness tracker that monitors physical activity, heart rate, sleep patterns, and overall health.

- ✦ **Fiverr** – An online marketplace connecting freelancers with clients for a variety of services, from graphic design to writing.

- ✦ **Google Fit** – A health and fitness tracking platform that encourages physical activity and wellness through data monitoring.

- ✦ **Google Home** – A smart speaker and home assistant that manages tasks, controls smart home devices, and provides information.

- ✦ **Gumroad** – A platform that allows creators to sell digital products, memberships, and courses directly to consumers.

- ✦ **Healow** – A health management app that enables users to access medical records, schedule appointments, and track health data.

- ✦ **Hostfully** – A vacation rental management platform that automates bookings, guest communication, and payments across Airbnb, Vrbo, and other platforms to streamline operations and maximize revenue.

- ✦ **Lumosity** – A brain-training app with exercises designed to improve cognitive skills, memory, and attention.

- ✦ **MindMeister** – A digital mind-mapping tool for brainstorming, organizing ideas, and planning projects visually.

- ✦ **Mint** – A budgeting and financial management app that tracks expenses, creates budgets, and monitors investments.

- ✦ **MyChart** – A health app that allows users to view medical records, communicate with healthcare providers, and manage appointments.

- ✦ **MyFitnessPal** – A nutrition and fitness tracking app that helps users set goals, log meals, and monitor physical activity.

- ✦ **Rosetta Stone** – A language-learning software that uses immersive, interactive methods to teach new languages.

- ✦ **Shopify** – An e-commerce platform that enables users to build and manage their own online stores.

- ✦ **Skillshare** – An online learning community focused on creative and business skills through classes led by professionals.

- ✦ **Teachable** – A platform for creating and selling online courses, with tools for content management, student engagement, and payment processing.

- ✦ **TripAdvisor** – A travel planning platform offering user reviews, recommendations, and booking options for destinations and activities.

- ✦ **Upwork** – An online platform connecting freelancers with clients seeking various services, including writing, design, and technical support.
- ✦ **VRBO** – A vacation rental marketplace where users can book short-term stays in private homes and unique accommodations.
- ✦ **WhatsApp** – A messaging app for text, voice, and video communication, as well as media sharing.
- ✦ **Words with Friends** – A popular online word game for social, turn-based competition with friends.
- ✦ **WooCommerce** – An open-source e-commerce plugin for WordPress that allows users to build and manage online stores.
- ✦ **YouTube** – A video-sharing platform providing content for learning, entertainment, and sharing user-generated videos.

Glossary of Key Terms

- ✦ **Active Engagement** – Pursuing activities and relationships that enhance personal satisfaction and emotional health.
- ✦ **Active Income** – Income earned from direct involvement in work, such as part-time jobs, consulting, or freelancing.
- ✦ **Adaptability** – The ability to adjust effectively to new situations, particularly important in retirement.
- ✦ **Adaptation** – The ongoing process of adjusting to lifestyle changes during retirement.
- ✦ **Aging in Place** – The ability to continue living independently and comfortably at home as one grows older.
- ✦ **Assessment** – A structured evaluation of one's financial, physical, or emotional well-being.
- ✦ **Asset-Light** – A business model that relies on technology or partnerships rather than physical assets for operational efficiency.
- ✦ **Belief System** – A set of guiding principles that shape a person's values, actions, and worldview.
- ✦ **Boardroom** – A meeting space where a company's board of directors makes high-level decisions on strategy and policies.

+ **Brain Health** – The overall functioning and well-being of the brain, encompassing memory, cognition, and emotional health.

+ **Cognitive Engagement** – Participating in activities that stimulate mental acuity and keep the mind sharp.

+ **Community Engagement** – Actively participating in local initiatives to support community welfare and personal connection.

+ **Digital Shift** – Adopting a technology-centric lifestyle to improve communication, convenience, and connection.

+ **Empathy** – The capacity to understand and resonate with others' feelings and perspectives.

+ **Exercise** – Physical or mental activities aimed at improving physical health, mental clarity, and emotional well-being.

+ **Family Connections** – Emotional bonds and interactions that foster support and unity among family members.

+ **Generosity** – The readiness to give time, resources, or kindness to others without expecting anything in return.

+ **H-E-R-O Strategy** – A framework for retirement centered on Health, Engagement, Resilience, and Ownership of one's life.

+ **Health-Focused Apps** – Mobile applications that assist in monitoring and managing health and wellness.

+ **Institutional Knowledge** – Valuable insights and skills gained through experience within an organization or field.

+ **Kübler-Ross Transition Curve** — A model originally developed to describe the five stages of grief—Denial, Anger, Bargaining, Depression, and Acceptance—now widely used to explain how people emotionally adjust to major life changes, including retirement.

+ **Legacy Building** – Intentional actions aimed at creating a lasting, positive impact aligned with one's values and contributions.

+ **Neural Plasticity** – The brain's lifelong ability to adapt and reorganize itself in response to learning and experiences.

+ **Proactive Health Management** – Taking early, preventive actions to maintain and enhance health over time.

✦ **Real-Life Case Study** – A practical example that demonstrates a concept in a relatable, real-world context.

✦ **The Retirement Transition Framework (RTF)** – Developed by David J. Cook, this framework guides retirees through the psychological, social, and practical aspects of retirement, focusing on health, purpose, financial stability, adaptability, and relationships to foster a fulfilling post-career life.

✦ **Robo-Advisors** – Automated online platforms that manage investments using algorithms and financial strategies.

✦ **Self-Reflection** – A thoughtful examination of one's thoughts, emotions, and actions to foster personal insight and growth.

✦ **Social Isolation** – The state of having few social connections, which can impact mental and emotional health.

✦ **Sustainability** – Maintaining or improving lifestyle, health, and finances to support long-term well-being.

✦ **Technology Adaptation** – Integrating new technologies into everyday life to enhance efficiency and enjoyment.

✦ **Telemedicine** – Delivering healthcare services remotely through digital platforms, often for convenience and accessibility.

✦ **Well-Being** – A comprehensive sense of health, including physical, mental, and emotional aspects.

✦ **Wellness Monitoring** – Using digital tools to track and analyze health indicators for proactive care.

Top 20 Lessons from *Retirement Shock*

1. Retirement without purpose becomes prolonged idleness.

2. Identity loss is real—reinvention is the way forward.

3. Financial stability is your foundation, not your finish line.

4. Structure creates freedom; drifting creates frustration.

5. A successful retirement starts with asking better questions.

6. Purpose isn't found—it's built, one step at a time.

7. You don't need a new job—you need a new reason to get up.

8. Small daily habits lead to long-term fulfillment.

9. Emotional readiness is just as important as financial readiness.

10. The Retirement Transition Framework helps turn uncertainty into clarity.

11. Passion often hides in curiosity—follow it.

12. Serving others brings meaning and connection.

13. Letting go of your work identity is uncomfortable, but necessary.

14. Legacy isn't about wealth—it's about how you show up in life.

15. Deep relationships are more valuable than any retirement plan.

16. Tech-savviness helps keep you relevant, independent, and connected.

17. Health is the real wealth in retirement—protect it.

18. Change is inevitable—your response is what matters most.

19. Success in retirement is personal, not traditional.

20. You're not retiring—you're rewiring for your next great chapter

Value Add: Tools and Resources

📑 RTF Quick Reference – One-Page Summary

This page lists the 10 Retirement Transition Framework (RTF) steps with brief summaries.

RTF Step	Summary
1. Transitioning from Career to Retirement	Let go of old identities and mentally prepare for the shift.
2. Managing Your Finances	Ensure financial stability to support a fulfilling life.
3. Beyond Financial Planning	Discover and pursue a sense of purpose beyond money.
4. Embracing Change	Accept uncertainty and grow through transition.
5. Exploring New Passions	Turn curiosity into meaningful activities and hobbies.
6. Strengthening Relationships	Build deep, supportive connections with others.
7. Leaving a Legacy	Create impact and meaning that extends beyond you.
8. Staying Current with Technology	Engage with tools that empower learning and connection.
9. Prioritizing Health	Focus on physical, mental, and spiritual well-being.
10. Putting It All Together	Integrate all steps into a personalized retirement life plan.

🧠 Reflection Prompts for Each RTF Step

1. What part of your identity was most tied to your career, and how do you feel about letting it go?

2. Do you feel financially secure? What does 'enough' mean to you?

3. What brings you a sense of purpose today?

4. What personal changes have been the hardest to accept in retirement?

5. What's one thing you've always been curious to try?

6. Which relationships energize you—and which ones drain you?

7. What do you want to be remembered for?

8. What's one piece of technology that could improve your daily life?

9. What's one small health habit you could improve today?

10. What does a successful and meaningful retirement look like to you?

💬 Starting the Conversation: Book Club Questions

✦ What surprised you most about the emotional side of retirement?

✦ Which RTF step felt most relevant or challenging to you—and why?

✦ How has your definition of success changed since leaving your career?

✦ Which story in the book resonated most with your own journey?

✦ Do you see yourself exploring new passions, or refining existing ones?

✦ How do you plan to stay connected—both socially and technologically?

✦ What does legacy mean to you now compared to earlier in life?

✦ What's one small change you're inspired to make after reading this book?

🗒 Chapter-by-Chapter Action Plan

Chapter	Key Takeaway	Action Step
Chapter 1: Transitioning from Career	Understand identity loss and emotional adjustment.	Reflect on your career identity and what comes next.
Chapter 2: Managing Your Finances	Financial stability is foundational.	Review your retirement budget and financial goals.
Chapter 3: Beyond Financial Planning	Purpose matters as much as money.	Identify activities that bring meaning.
Chapter 4: Embracing Change	Change is inevitable— growth is optional.	Note one personal change you've embraced.
Chapter 5: Redefining Success	Retirement success isn't about achievement—it's about fulfillment.	List your new definition of success.
Chapter 6: Exploring New Passions	Curiosity leads to purpose.	Try a new class, hobby, or experience.
Chapter 7: Strengthening Relationships	Connection fuels well-being.	Reach out to someone meaningful this week.
Chapter 8: Leaving a Legacy	Legacy is about daily actions, not just end results.	Write down how you want to be remembered.
Chapter 9: Staying Current with Tech	Technology empowers retirement living.	Learn one new tech tool or app.
Chapter 10: Prioritizing Health	Health is wealth.	Commit to one health habit this week.

Retirement Transition Framework (RTF) Summary Worksheet

Step 1: Financial Stability as the Foundation

Evaluate your financial position and define what financial security looks like for you.

Your Notes / Actions:

Step 2: Letting Go of Old Identities & Embracing Change

Reflect on your career identity and explore ways to embrace your evolving self.

Your Notes / Actions:

Step 3: Redefining Success & Finding Fulfillment

Write down what success means to you now and how you want to feel fulfilled.

Your Notes / Actions:

Step 4: Exploring New Passions & Purpose

List interests or curiosities you want to explore more deeply in retirement.

Your Notes / Actions:

Step 5: Strengthening Relationships & Social Connections

Identify relationships you want to nurture and ways to expand your social circle.

Your Notes / Actions:

Step 6: Adapting to Technology & Lifelong Learning

Note technologies or subjects you want to learn to stay connected and stimulated.

Your Notes / Actions:

Step 7: Prioritizing Health & Well-Being

Document your goals for physical, mental, and spiritual health.

Your Notes / Actions:

Step 8: Leaving a Legacy - Making a Lasting Impact

Think about how you want to be remembered and contributions you want to make.

Your Notes / Actions:

Step 9: RTF in Action - My Plan in Motion

Summarize your top priorities and create a weekly or monthly routine to support them.

Your Notes / Actions: